Blossoming Autism

My Life With Autism and Sixteen Things I Wish People Knew

By Jillian Schmeltzer

Dedication

This book is dedicated to my parents, Joseph and Elaine Schmeltzer, for always supporting, understanding, and accepting me. Mom and Dad, you guys are the reason I have reached this lifelong dream of writing a book. You have consistently fought for me and made sure I had everything I needed. Above all else, you have helped me blossom into the person I am today. I truly don't know where I would be without you. Thank you for all that you have ever done for me. I love you!

"Keep your face always towards the sunshine and shadows will fall behind you."

Walt Whitman

Table of Contents

Foreword   Page 7

Introduction   Page 9

Chapter One: Going Unnoticed   Page 13
Don't be afraid of a diagnosis. It opens up so many doors.

Chapter Two: The Pink Bedroom   Page 19
As we grow, some things will change and some will stay the same.

Chapter Three: Walking In Squares   Page 29
Emotions often drive the behaviors in good ways and bad.

Chapter Four: Elephant Alphabet   Page 39
Some things that are easy for you are hard for us and things that
are easy for us are hard for you.

Chapter Five: Flower Patch   Page 47
What you see is not what you get.
There is a lot more than what meets the eye.

Chapter Six: Black Scribbles   Page 55
Crying is learning and crying is growth. All we need is patience.

Chapter Seven: Dealing The Emotion Cards   Page 65
It is okay to take a break. We need time to reset.

Chapter Eight: Scissor Cutting   Page 77
We learn in a different way.
Sometimes, we need a little bit more coaching.

Chapter Nine: Drop And Give Me Twenty   Page 87
If you know it will happen, if you think it might happen,
or if you want it to happen, just be prepared.

Chapter Ten: French Fry Feelings　　　　　　Page 100
If it doesn't work, you haven't found the right strategy yet. Don't get too discouraged. We want to improve just as much as you want us to.

Chapter Eleven: Hockey Puck　　　　　　　　Page 113
Just because you can't see it doesn't mean it isn't there.
We have to adapt everyday and sometimes we also need to be adapted for.

Chapter Twelve: Knight In Shining Armor　　　Page 126
It always depends on every aspect of the situation. If it works once, it might not work the next time.

Chapter Thirteen: Unplug The Microwave　　　Page 139
Things change and we will learn how to cope in our own ways.
What is an issue now will not be an issue forever.

Chapter Fourteen: Special Problems　　　　　Page 152
Come into our world. Even if it seems as though our door is shut, it isn't. We have a lot more to offer than you realize.

Chapter Fifteen: The Drop Of A Hat　　　　　Page 166
People with autism can and will accomplish great things.
You just have to take it one step at a time and not worry too much about falling behind.

Chapter Sixteen: Step On It　　　　　　　　Page 174
There are many different perceptions in this world.
Don't let them define you. Speak your wisdom and teach instead.

Foreword

By Melissa Bishop

"Flowers don't worry about how they're going to bloom. They just open up and turn toward the light and that makes them beautiful." - Jim Carrey

Sometimes the flower can have a difficult time reaching the light. There may be other flowers, weeds, or even a tree keeping the flower shaded and unable to bloom to its fullest potential. But nonetheless the flower will find a way to grow. It may grow unlike the other flowers. It may lean a little to the left. But it will grow! And beautiful it will be!

I met Jillian when she entered my class in 6th grade. She was very shy. I asked her what she was most concerned about entering middle school, but she didn't answer. Her mother informed me that Jillian was most concerned about being late, walking into a classroom and being stared at by everyone. I assured Jillian we would change that quickly! She didn't respond, but the look she gave me said, "Good luck. I am not changing." From that moment on, it became my goal to get Jillian to push beyond her comfort zone and to enter into the gray area she so feared.

Blossoming Autism is a wonderful autobiography and insight into the mind of a young woman's journey through the black and white world of autism. Jillian is an exceptional writer and has written a book that allows the reader to experience all the joys and pain of living with autism. Her gift of the written word to illustrate her world will make one laugh and cry at the same time as though one is experiencing it with her.

I have been teaching for 15 years and in education for 25. I have had the privilege of teaching many exceptional students, but none as extraordinary as Jillian. Through her career as a student, I have begged Jillian to write her experiences down, pleaded with her to speak as an advocate for others, and urged her to love and accept herself for who she is. She is finally working through her anxieties, freeing her mind, and allowing others a glimpse into her world. I am so proud of her for blossoming and growing into the beautiful flower she is.

Introduction

"Nineteen year old girl with autism writes book." It was an article sent to me by one of my teacher friends, Mr. Pfaff. When I read the headline, it seemed like fate. At the time, I was a nineteen year old girl with autism thinking about writing a book, just getting used to my second semester of college and entering the world of adulthood. No longer am I a child with autism. I am in an area unknown to me, a place I have never really been before. I know what I want to do, but I don't know how it is going to happen. I know what I want out of life, but I am starting to see the extra hurdles I will have to cross to get there. I am in a very unique situation and I am having to focus so much more on every little baby step that I take. Sitting on the floor of my parents' bedroom, my phone buzzed next to me. Mr. Pfaff had sent me an attachment. Curious what it could be, I quickly opened the message not knowing it would start a fire in me that had laid dormant for the last few years. I wanted to be that headline and I knew I could do it.

When I was in sixth grade, I had a particular amount of trouble with school. I was constantly nervous and I never wanted to go. It was like the first time you drop your kid off at preschool and they don't want you to leave. Except I was twelve and getting dropped off at middle school. I had started out the year very strong but, when February hit, I had lost it. I couldn't put my finger on what I was so afraid of; I just knew the thought of school brought instant fear to me. Middle school is a rough transition for everyone, and I think the differences that started to take place in the way my peers interacted with each other and presented themselves was too much for me to handle. It was a big change and I had a really hard time getting used to it. My autism was also something that I masked everyday and it was getting harder and harder to do so.

Once spring came along, they had tried everything to get me to feel more comfortable. My mom was starting a new job and it probably exhausted her to drop me off every day. My new Special Education teachers, Mr. Pfaff and Mrs. Bishop, seemed to understand me more than I understood myself. They tried walking me into class and shutting the door behind me. They began to let me get picked up early every day so the day wasn't as long. Most days, I spent my first two classes in their room instead of my English class where I was supposed to be. On the really bad days, they let me go home, having only been on campus about thirty minutes. I was a mess that year and I was getting really frustrated at my situation. I was at my grandparent's house one evening, which is right next door to the house I grew up in, when I found myself in front of the computer. It was the spring of 2012 and I was twelve years old. My parents were running errands and I wanted badly to express how I felt, so I decided to write:

"I'm Jillian Schmeltzer. You can call me Jillz, Jillster, Lil Schmeltzer, Jill Pill, Jillbean, I don't care. Anyway, I have autism. That means I have trouble being social or expressing myself to others. If I know the person well, then it's different but otherwise, it is hard for me. In little situations, I have added stress. At least that's what it seems like. Something can happen to me that won't bother anybody but it's the end of the world for me. For example, one of my friends could get irritated with me. For most people, they will just say "They'll get over it," but for me I have to fix it because I hate to upset anyone. I wish that didn't happen but it does. That's just me. Anyway, my teacher, Mrs. Bishop, is someone who understands me like she's known me her whole life. Really it hasn't even been a year but she and I are really close. I look up to her. I'm really lucky to have her. I can have a problem at school with friends and she always knows what to say. She really isn't my teacher. She is more like my friend. Even though she teaches me math sometimes, she understands me. I love that about her. She has a really good friend that also teaches special education and he helps me out too. His name is Mr. Pfaff. I'm not as close to him, but I look up to him the same way. He understands me too. Anyway, I have been having trouble going to school for the past few weeks and I don't really have a clue why. They say it's a pattern in my brain that I have to break and that may be true but I feel differently about it. I feel that I'm being pressured. Like I'm being forced to do something that I don't want to do. I know that they aren't forcing me to do anything but that's just how I feel. I feel sad every night before school because I know I'm going to have to go in sad or not. That is what they have to do though or else it won't get better. I know they are just trying to help me overcome this and I want to because I know it's better for me and Mrs. Bishop, Mr. Pfaff, and my mom. She tries to help me too. I figured I'd give her some credit for not losing her patience on me and helping me too. Anyway, I feel like when I cry in the morning before school, I put stress on my mom and make her feel bad. I don't want to and that's never my intention. And maybe even Mrs. Bishop because sometimes when I am having trouble I don't go to my 1st and 2nd period classes and I stay with her for those classes. Even though I have English for 1st and 2nd period, it's still two periods. Anyway, when I don't go to 1st and 2nd, I stay with her in the resource room. For some reason, it makes me feel comfortable to be with her and know that I don't have to go to English. I feel like when I stay with her, it makes it harder on her because then not only does she have a class to teach, but she has me to worry about. She tells me not to worry about that but I still think about it that way. They have tried many things to get me back into the pattern of going into English in the morning but none have worked for me. They have tried just leaving me there and making me go in but when all those people (my classmates) come out of the classroom, it annoys me. I know they're trying to make me feel better but it still annoys me. That also doesn't work because when they leave me there, they think that I will go in and that will help me overcome it but really I don't know what to do. It makes me feel confused. They have also tried a break at lunch where I get to do my rope and my music. I liked that. It made me feel ready to finish out my day but these past few days, I haven't really needed it. I feel fine without it but for some reason, my break didn't make my mornings go better. At this point, I don't know what will. They are doing a thing where I could spend one day a week in the resource room and last week, I should've thought it over a little better. I don't like Thursdays. They are never good for me and last week, I used Tuesday as my day in the resource room but I had more problems on Thursday. I ended up staying with Mr. Pfaff, who was principal for the day, in the office. I felt better not going to English but I don't know how to make myself go. It has to happen sooner or later though. :-) -Jillian"

I printed out the paper and gave it to my grandma to read. She was amazed and I was amazed that she was amazed. When my parents got home, she gave it to my mom and then she was amazed. I didn't know what was so great about it, but she made me print out a few more copies, and she took them to Mr. Pfaff and Mrs. Bishop and all of the other adults who had been working with me. They all sat me down and told me how amazing it was that I had written this.

I didn't realize at the time that what I wanted so badly was to be able to communicate what I was feeling. It is a part of my autism that was always such a struggle and I have really had to learn to cope with it over the years. Knowing what I want to say, but feeling like I can't say it. Knowing what it is that's bothering me, but not being able to express that, which only makes the situation worse. At that time, I knew I had autism, and I knew I had certain struggles that my peers didn't have. However, I didn't yet know enough about autism to know that I had SO MUCH to say, but I just couldn't get it out. I didn't know that by writing this paper, I was letting people into my mind where they so badly wanted to go. They so badly wanted to understand why I was having such a hard time and I didn't know this was going to be so helpful.

Ever since then, I have written a paper every time I feel stuck, every time I feel like I can't explain my feelings verbally, every time I want people to please understand me and how I am feeling. I just open up a document and I write. I type really fast. The thoughts just roll off the tips of my fingers instead of my tongue. It is a gift I was given and I want to pursue it in amazing ways. A lot of the things I may cover are uncomfortable for me to write about. They bring up difficult memories or they open me up to a lot of vulnerabilities. However, I know that by going forward and writing about my experiences, it will be helpful to somebody. So I will write for the ones who come after me, the ones who find themselves lost in the criteria, and the ones who just can't get their thoughts out. I have autism and this is my story.

Chapter One: Going Unnoticed

Don't be afraid of a diagnosis. It opens up so many doors.

I was diagnosed with autism spectrum disorder when I had just turned eight. It was October 2, 2007 and I remember it vividly. I didn't know what I was at the doctor for exactly, but I had a subtle understanding of it at the same time. I knew I was different from the other kids my age. I knew I had quirks the other kids didn't have. I knew I got more upset than they did, and I knew I felt things a little bit differently. It is interesting to me that even though I didn't have a clear diagnosis yet, I seemed to know that I had autism. I have always had memories of that final doctor's appointment and years later when I found out that was the day I was diagnosed, I was shocked. I thought I was a baby when I was diagnosed; I thought I had known about it my whole life. It goes to show I have always had an inkling I was not the same. I think I knew, even at a really young age, that some of the things I did were not necessarily normal, and they were being questioned by everyone around me.

I remember a lot about that day. I remember building a marble tower in the waiting room with my mom and my cousin, Melissa, who is also my godmother. I remember showing the doctor my rope and feeling embarrassed. I remember being taken out of that room and hanging out with the receptionist while my mom got the final diagnosis that had taken her years to get. I remember walking outside with the receptionist and taping a paper up on the door. This doctor had just gotten a billboard put up in town that advertised her office, and this paper displayed a picture of it for her to see when she came out that night. I remember reuniting with my mom a little while later, and I remember driving out of the parking lot when it was all over.

Over the previous couple of years leading up to that day, I had been misdiagnosed with a few other things. I had been diagnosed with Obsessive-Compulsive Disorder, Sensory Integration Disorder, and Stereotypic Movement Disorder. I guess they weren't necessarily a misdiagnosis. They were a diagnosis of things autistic people may have, and I probably do have, but I wasn't being diagnosed with autism itself, which is what I definitely have. I had gone to many different doctors all over the state of California, I had taken many different tests, and I had been looked at quizzically by lots of different people. I was a mystery; nobody knew why I did the things I did. Even twelve years ago, people didn't know as much about autism as they do today. They would look at a little girl like me who appeared fine on the outside, but exhibited very odd behaviors, and they would try to give their best guess. But that didn't stop my mom from pushing through. When she received the final diagnosis of autism, she was certain that, at last, it was the right diagnosis. It was the blanket over all of the other things I was diagnosed with. It was the root cause of all of these underlying struggles and disabilities. My mom didn't give up, she fought for me, and she got me what I needed. She knew me better than anyone, and she knew that there was something different about me. I am so thankful that she did.

I am my mom's fourth child and her second girl. She is a preschool teacher and has been for many years. When I started to show signs that I was different, she noticed it right away. A lot of autistic people have fallen through the cracks in terms of a diagnosis and a lot of people still will. This is because autism is not visible on the outside and every person is so different that you can't determine whether or not they have autism based on a few small facts, such as eye contact. Some people with autism make great eye contact, some make little to no eye contact, and others might make too much eye contact. The differences are so vast that many people have not received a proper diagnosis of autism well into adulthood. I was lucky.

Some people may think getting an actual diagnosis of autism is unfortunate and disappointing. Some parents may feel hopeless and come to the conclusion their child won't be able to do any of the things other children will do. But I am thankful I got a diagnosis of autism because a diagnosis is a privilege. Autism is a part of who I am. It is something that makes me just that: me. It brings a lot of challenge to my life, but the challenge is explained because I have a diagnosis of autism. I received help because I have a diagnosis of autism. I was able to understand myself and learn how to best jump over all of these hurdles life has thrown my way because I have a diagnosis of autism. Without it, I would be completely clueless as to what is causing me to have these struggles. I would have gone through school without help, understanding, or intervention. I would have felt hopeless. I wouldn't have been able to work on myself the way I have. Autism doesn't go away. That is a true and sometimes cringeworthy statement. But I have already learned how to cope with having autism in so many ways because I understand it and I know how it affects me. Everyone has a different view of autism that is dependent upon who they have encountered and what they have experienced. Every autistic person is vastly different, yet similar in some ways. Autism goes unnoticed a lot of the time. People don't see the thoughts or the struggles. That is the way it is for a lot of autistic people. All you have to do is look a little bit harder and you will see it.

I had an appointment at the University of San Francisco Complex Case Clinic on March 1, 2005, about two and a half years before my official diagnosis. They put me in a room with mirrors where I did my rope, which is my form of stimming. I didn't know they were there. I couldn't see them, but they could all see me. It was an abnormal movement, they said, but they didn't know why I did it. It surely wasn't normal, but it was unexplainable. There was blood drawn. There was an attempt at an MRI. There were cameras set up in my bedroom to film the things I did when I was alone. There were weekly appointments. But there was no explanation. My pediatrician was wonderful, but she didn't think there was anything more to the story. What my mom had already heard was all that she was going to get. When I would visit my pediatrician or any other doctor, I would smile, I would laugh, and I would make eye contact. I didn't share my thoughts with anyone at that time in my life simply because I didn't think they mattered. I didn't know anyone would care to know about everything that was going on in my brain. I didn't think there was anything unique about the way I thought about things. A few days after that final appointment, my mom was at my brother's basketball game, and she got a phone call from my pediatrician. She had referred us to a clinical psychiatrist as a last case scenario who was able to give an actual diagnosis. My mom walked out of the gym and into the hallway where she answered the phone. My pediatrician told her she had just talked to the clinical psychiatrist, and she was pretty sure I had autism spectrum disorder. They were the words my mom had been looking for. She wasn't necessarily hoping to hear it, but it was an answer to all of the hopelessly unanswered questions she had.

Being misdiagnosed (or taking a long time to get the officially correct diagnosis) was the first time in my life I would be misunderstood in terms of my autism. Some of the misconceptions I deal with on a larger scale are that I am being dramatic, and that I don't have anything to say. To people who don't have autism, it can seem as such. They can't see what I am thinking or how I am feeling. All they see is me and, to them, I am normal. I don't look like I have anything wrong with me. My disability is an invisible disability and, with that being said, half of the battle is other people. When I am feeling really anxious or I have a meltdown, other people don't always understand what that means. To them, I am being a dramatic girl. It isn't unusual to be such, and I am definitely not exempt from dramatic moments. However, I am different. I don't have the ability to verbally say what I need to say with ease. It takes a lot of extra work for me to express what is bothering me and to get help in return. Every time I have had a meltdown, the reason is that I can't gather all of my thoughts and cohesively put them into words. I have fallen apart before because I knew nobody understood what I was trying to say and, therefore, I wasn't going to get the help I really needed. The fact I have autism is not an excuse to behave a certain way, and there have been times where I have reacted unnecessarily due to other causes, such as hormones or, yes, drama. But most of the time, I feel embarrassed about acting a certain way because I know my autism is the unseen reality of the situation for everyone else. Those are the times when I wish people could see it. Having the kind of autism I have means that I am expected to conform in a world that isn't made up of people like me. I am having to mask vital parts of what makes me the person I am, even to those very close to me, and I am required to change the parts that just don't make sense to other people. Half of the battle *is* other people because I am an autistic person living in a world that doesn't recognize me as such.

Most of the people around me would consider me to be a shy person. That is not an unusual thing for a girl my age and I definitely have shy tendencies. I am a quiet person, and I get very nervous in new and different situations. Then, when I am nervous, I kind of put all of my guards up and I am afraid to talk. I am scared of saying or doing the wrong thing so I just keep quiet. What is misunderstood about it, though, is it appears as though I don't have anything to say. And maybe sometimes, I don't have anything to offer to the conversation. But most of the time, I have so many things I want to say, but I just don't know how to put it into words. Sometimes I spend so much time trying to think up a follow-up question or a response to what someone has just said to me, by the time I think of one, the conversation has already moved on to another topic. Or maybe sometimes I am too wrapped up in the things going on in my own mind that I am distracted from the conversation. It seems as though I am not paying attention when, really, I am gathering my thoughts, or I am trying to think up ways to engage in the conversation. When I am in class, I never raise my hand or volunteer to do anything. I just like to sit back and observe. I don't want the attention on me. However, I usually have answers to the questions being asked or an opinion on the subject being discussed. I am just too afraid to say it, but it may look like I am disinterested or I don't know the answer. My junior year of high school, I was in my history class and my teacher asked everyone who the Vice President is. At the time, it was Joe Biden, and I have grown up in a politically knowledgeable enough family to know that one for sure. I remember only one person raised their hand, and I looked around shocked. I was like, "All of these people don't know who the Vice President is?!" After I thought about it, I realized I knew who it was and I didn't raise my hand either. I probably wasn't the only one who did that. Then, I regretted not raising my hand because I was like, "I knew the answer! I could have looked smart if I only would have raised my hand!" That is just a mild example of a time where I have not said what I was thinking out of fear of everyone looking at me when it might have actually been a beneficial moment to open my mouth. I can be my own worst enemy in this way.

Because of these common misconceptions, I can understand why I was misdiagnosed, or not diagnosed with the correct thing right away. I was on the right track in terms of academics. I actually talked earlier than most children. I was able to get around, and I could hold conversations with people if necessary. Typically, when I was younger, it was a really awkward conversation; however, it was a conversation nonetheless. But when I got overstimulated or upset, I shut down. Communication basically vanished and it took a lot of prodding to find out what I was sad about. Things that seemed easy to some people seemed like a huge task for me. I had my thoughts organized into categories, and I was memorizing everything as I went through the day. I had a tense feeling pulsing through my body every couple of hours that indicated I needed to do my rope and my music and it didn't go away until I did. Those are the things people didn't see when they observed me. It was all hidden and it always has been for my entire life. Nobody can see it, and therefore, I have to tell about it.

Chapter Two: The Pink Bedroom

As we grow, some things will change and some will stay the same.

I have something I call my rope. It is how I stim. Stimming is defined as behavior consisting of repetitive actions or movements displayed by people with developmental disorders, most typically those on the autism spectrum. People stim in a lot of different ways and some stims can be subtle and unnoticeable, while others are very distinct and different. I have done my rope my entire life. My rope has gone through many different stages and it is essential to me. I cannot get through the day without doing my rope. There have been times where I was on vacation with my family and my rope time has gotten cut short. Most times, that leads to a meltdown or something very close to it until I can get my hands on my rope. Usually, I do it for an hour at a time a few times a day depending on how busy I am that particular day.

My rope is a long piece of fleece cut from a blanket. When I do my rope, I run my hands through the fleece, twirl it, and make a humming noise. While doing so, I am processing all kinds of information and my mind is going a million miles a minute. Physically, my hands are moving very fast along with my mind. My knees lock and my upper body moves in vigorous ways. I have difficulty with my joints in my knees and my shoulders from spending so much time doing my rope. Upon inspecting my hands, you will see calluses and blisters that first formed years ago but have never gone away due to constantly being run over. Just recently, I have started having back spasms every few seconds while I do my rope. It is straining on my body, but there is no other option for me. I need it, physically and mentally, to get through my day. Though it is hard on my body, it is a form of exercise for me. I always get very out of breath and sometimes I end up nearly shirtless because I get so hot when I do my rope. For some neurological reason, my ears and cheeks turn bright red and I sweat profusely. If I get a sore throat, I have to take into consideration the fact that I have been making a humming noise with my voice non-stop for an hour before I jump to other conclusions. And, yes, I have gone through times when I was little having to use a dry erase board to communicate. I still occasionally get a hoarse voice and have to take a break, especially during the summer when I have more time on my hands to do my rope.

The first stage my rope went through did not involve a rope. I made my humming sound and I would wring/flap my hands. I held them out in front of me with my arms very stiff, and I turned my hands back and forth. It was like a mixture of wringing and flapping and twisting. Typically, I would wring them in front of the television, or I would stand at the refrigerator and stare at the pictures on it as I did this. This was one of the first signs my parents had that there was something a little different about me. I was about a year old when I first started doing this and, at the time, they didn't know why I did it. My grandma has told me they used to watch me standing at the fridge, and they would all comment on how cute it was. I have a video from my second birthday where my siblings and my cousins surprised me. I was walking through my grandparent's kitchen and into their living room where everyone was sitting. In the video, I ran through the room wringing my hands and when everyone yelled, "SURPRISE!!" I was scared and ran right back out the door. They didn't know at the time I was so engrossed in the thoughts going through my mind that it was going to be so startling for me. They just thought it was a cute and quirky little kid behavior I had. Now, when I watch that video, I know exactly what I was doing. For some reason, the rigid motion I was making with my hands was very satisfying for me, and it was all that I had before I discovered what is now my rope.

Even though my rope involves so much physical movement, my mind is actually doing the most work when I do my rope. The physical part of it goes hand in hand with the mental part and it enhances the experience of the stim for me. When I would wring my hands to a movie, I was actually memorizing it. I have always loved words and pictures and putting them together is fascinating to me. It is almost like second nature at this point. When I would wring my hands while staring at the pictures on the fridge, I was memorizing the pictures. I now have thousands and thousands of pictures lined up in my head in a pretty specific order, and when I do my rope, I am putting words onto the pictures. Even at such a young age, that is what I was doing. At that time, I didn't have a wide variety of pictures. It was basically only limited to pictures of family members I saw on the fridge or in frames around the house. While staring at the T.V. screen, my mind was able to see the pictures that were on the fridge (without actually seeing them physically) and put the words being said in the movie onto the pictures in my mind. I still do this exact same thing to this day just in different ways. The process in my mind is 1) I hear the words being spoken, 2) I see the pictures in my head in a specific order (the order they were presented on the fridge when I was little), 3) I put the words being said onto the picture, 4) I listen for the next sentence, and I move my mind to the next picture in order.

The next phase my rope went through became a little bit more physical. I realized I liked how it felt to run something through my hands. Growing up, my grandparents, Norman and Dian, lived right next door to me, and when my parents worked (before I started school), I stayed with them for the day. At the time, my grandma was taking care of her mom, my Grandma Howard, who was in her nineties. She stayed in what we call the pink bedroom, given that name because of all of the pink fixtures, pink wallpaper, pink decorations, and a pink chair where my Grandma Howard sat. I would spend hours in there with her, and one of the things I fell in love with was her metal necklace. I would sit on her lap and read books and, one day, I started running my hands through her necklace. She would take it off and give it to me, and I would walk around the room running it through my fingers and making my traditional humming noise. I would open up a book and be able to process the pictures I would see. This became another way for me to do my rope because now I was exposed to even more words and pictures. I would take her necklace out to the fridge and run it through my fingers as I looked at the pictures or watched T.V. There is an old picture of me asleep on my Grandma Howard's lap and you can see her necklace sprawled across my legs. I always wanted it with me and it became almost like a comfort item for me. Quickly, just wringing my hands became a thing of the past because now I had discovered how wonderful it was to be able to physically feel the touch of something as I did my rope. It intensified the feeling I got from doing my rope, and the physical part has done that for me ever since.

When I was about four, my rope changed up again. This is when it earned the name "my rope." I started to run my fingers through an actual tying rope that my grandpa had outside by the pool. It's job was to pull the pool cover onto the water when everyone was done swimming for the day. I don't know what exactly made me start to use it; I just know that I must've liked the feel of it. It was obviously a lot more rough of a texture and I think that possibly could have been more satisfying for me. However, because it was a really rough material, it gave me a lot of blisters, cuts, and burns, but I didn't care. I needed to do it. This was about the time where I started to do my rope to the conversations of people around me. I would stand in the pool area while my grandparents, cousins, siblings, and parents swam and chatted, and I would stim to the words they were saying. I would make my humming noise and run my fingers through the rope. I would think of the pictures on the fridge, and I would put the words they were saying onto the pictures in my head. By doing this, I created a long line of pictures categorized and chronologically placed in my mind, and I went through them multiple times a day. I have always been very organized with the pictures. I have always had them in a very specific order, and whenever I saw new ones I just added them into my line of pictures. Sometimes if I was doing my rope to a conversation and someone didn't remember what was said, I could trace my mind back to the picture the words were said on and be able to tell them what they said. Having the order they were in memorized made it possible to backtrack and recall what was said in the conversation. I was putting the words onto the pictures and I was memorizing it as I went.

A little while later, my rope started to do a little too much damage to my hands, so my mom came up with a method for me to try out that was a lot more gentle. I began to use the tie on my grandpa's bathrobe. My mom took the tie out of her robe and gave it to me to use specifically as my new rope when I was at home. When I was at my grandparents' house, I would run to their closet and get the tie out of my grandpa's robe first thing. My grandpa actually still doesn't have a tie on his bathrobe because I used it as my rope when I was little. I would do the same thing with the bathrobe ties that I did with the wringing of the hands, the necklace, and the rope. I went through the pictures and put words on them whether it be from the television, a book, or a conversation I was listening to.

Eventually, I discovered the type of rope that I still use to this day. For Christmas one year, my sister Lindsey made my brothers Ethan and Austin blankets that represented their favorite football teams. She also made one specific to our hometown. One side of the blanket was blue and the other was white, which are our school colors. She had quite a bit of fabric left over and my mom cut it up into long pieces and I began to use that as my rope. Today, I still have that blanket just for this specific reason. I have had many blue and white ropes over the years. My rope usually lasts about two years before I will need a new one. I run it through my hands for long periods of time every single day, so after awhile, it gets very worn out and it will snap in half. I am always right in the middle of doing my rope when it happens. However, that is all right because I have that blanket available to cut off another piece and begin using it. I typically have a hard time adjusting to a new rope because it will feel a lot different than the one I had previously. It will be very soft and thick until I have used it for a couple of days and it starts to wear down a little. For some reason, the rougher texture is what I like better. My mom had tried at one point to find me a new rope at a fabric store before my sister made those blankets and after I had snapped her bathrobe tie. The one she got me was a lot softer and it did not work the same. When I say that, it's really what I mean. The texture affected my ability to actually be able to stim. It was too soft. I definitely preferred having a rougher texture, which is what I got with my sister's blankets. If I don't have the right physical portion of the stim, then the mental part won't work as well.

I wish I could tell you why my rope is so important to me or why, out of all things in the world, this is what I do to stim. But I don't know why. All I know is it is essential to me. I have to do my rope every single day or I will start to get agitated and, eventually, I will fall apart. Often times, people assume I just want to do my rope because it is something I enjoy doing. Though I do love to do my rope, it is not as simple as just wanting to do it. It is a feeling I get in my body, a tenseness that just keeps building up in me until I can release it by doing my rope. I often compare it to being hungry. When you're hungry, you know you're hungry because you get a feeling in your body that lets you know you're hungry. A lot of people like to eat, but you also have to eat in order to live, and the feeling and your overall well-being will only get worse and worse the longer you go without eating. It is the same thing. When I start to get that tense feeling, I have to let it out or it will get worse. However, there are many times when I am unable to physically do my rope at that exact moment. For example, when I am at work or school, I can't do my rope. When I have a really long day with hardly any downtime, such as my senior trip, I can't do my rope. Those kinds of days can be extremely hard for me. Sometimes, if there is a lot going on and I am busy, I won't be thinking about it as much so I won't feel completely plagued by the feeling. For example, when I am spending the day at an amusement park, all the excitement of everything going on will make me kind of forget about it for awhile. But then when I sit down to eat, the feeling will hit me full force, and it can really put a damper on the time I am having and the same can be said for the people around me. When my mind is not being stimulated enough, the feeling tends to take over. It makes what would be really fun days, like one spent at an amusement park, a lot less fun, especially as the day goes on. Little things that normally don't annoy me that much will make me ANGRY and noises that don't typically get to me will start to be a lot harder for me to handle.

To combat this problem, I have worked out a way to be able to do my rope without anyone knowing what I am doing. I can do it in my head. This doesn't have the same effect that physically doing my rope has, but it can work for a period of time. Usually when I do it, I have some sort of physical stimulation as well. I typically will rub my fingers together, or occasionally I will have a firm grip on my pencil if I'm in class and it just gives me a little bit more fulfillment in the physical way. Typically when I am at school, I will listen to the words the teacher is saying and I will put them on pictures I have in my head. Now that I am older and I have social media, I see a lot more pictures than I used to. I see pictures of almost everyone I know and, yes, I memorize them. I will look at a lot of people's profiles on different social media sites just to memorize their pictures. It sounds really creepy when I say it like that, but it is part of how I do my rope. I memorize pictures and I put words on them. It's just what I do and my logic is the more pictures I have memorized, the better. As a result, I accidentally hit the "like" button on a lot of people's pictures from a really long time ago and it's embarrassing.

Anyway, when I am in class, I will put the words the teacher is saying on these pictures as they speak. Like I said, I have thousands of pictures in my mind in a specific order and once I feel like I have enough words on the picture, I will move onto the next picture. It sounds really confusing to most people when I tell them this information but, for me, it is actually fairly easy to keep track of what I am doing. I organize it in my head by doing things such as only putting two sentences on each picture. I have different categories of pictures based on who is in the picture or where the picture was taken, so while I do have one big long chain of pictures, I also have them placed in different areas of my mind depending upon these factors. Sometimes it is dependent upon the facial expressions of the people in the picture, the background, or the amount of people in it. A lot of times, though, it is based on the people in the picture or the setting of the picture.

If I see a new picture of someone on Facebook, for example, I will put that picture in a specific place in my mind where it "matches" the pictures around it. It doesn't just go to the back of the line; it is given a place. I typically have an area for almost everyone I know in my head and their pictures are in their area. But sometimes, I have areas based on other things. For example, if I see a picture on Facebook of someone at the beach, I may not put that picture in that person's area. Instead, I may put it in the area where there are a lot of pictures of people at the beach. They are all in one huge order, but they also have their own spots, if that makes any sense. In other words, when I do my rope in my head, I can almost make it less complicated for myself because of the way I have the pictures organized. I do sometimes get bored going through my pictures in my head in the same order every single time, so I will occasionally spice it up a little bit. I will continue to go through the order, but I may decide to do my rope to the pictures that have, for example, two people in them and then, when I am done, go back to the beginning and go through the ones that only have one person in them. After that, I will go through the ones with multiple people in them. That is just an example of a way I will challenge myself a little bit more with my rope so it isn't *always* in the same order. It usually takes me a couple weeks to get through all of the pictures and start over again. And, to be more specific, I only have pictures in my head that have people in them. I obviously see pictures on social media that do not have people in them, but I don't make the effort to memorize those.

When I did my rope in my head in all of these ways during school, I was getting enough fulfillment of my rope to get me through the school day. Now, it is enough to get me through a couple hours of class. The only downside to it is I will sometimes be paying more attention to what is going on in my head than the words actually coming out of the teacher's mouth. As a result, I occasionally miss things, but it is rare. I can usually take in what the teacher is saying while still doing my rope in my head. However, I kind of know this has the potential of being a problem, so I have come up with ways to make it easier for me. I have certain words I will be listening for and, when the teacher says them, I will put them onto whatever picture I am on in my head. For example, I will use if/then statements or proper nouns. I will wait for the teacher to use one of these statements or words, and then I will put whatever they said onto the picture and then I will wait until I hear it again. That is kind of a way I have made it possible to not get completely distracted with what is going on in my mind while also being able to get a little bit of my rope in when it isn't physically available to me.

The times doing my rope in my head does not work at all is when I am having one on one conversations. I used to try to do that when I was in middle school. I was extra stressed then, and the more stressed out I am, the more I need to do my rope, so I was just trying to cope. But I started to realize I would take way too long to process what the other person was saying because I was more focused on doing my rope in my head than I was about having a conversation. Therefore, it took me way longer than socially acceptable to respond to what someone had just said. I would hear their words, let my mind go to where my pictures are, remember what picture I was on, think about the words that had just been said to me, put them on the pictures, and then regain my focus and think of how to respond to their statement. I eventually had to tell myself that was too much, and I needed to limit it to when I wasn't being directly talked to and nobody was expecting a response from me. When I am in a group setting and nobody is talking to me specifically, I will usually be doing my rope in my head. No one knows that is what I am doing, and it is a way for me to cope with being without my rope for a period of time. That is part of the way I am misunderstood. It seems as though I have nothing to add to the conversation, but really I might just be deeply engrossed in the pictures in my head because I am trying to make it through the day.

One thing I know about my rope is it does not seem normal to a lot of people. It actually seems very weird and unexplainable. That is why my rope is something I keep very private. When I was little, I used to do my rope out in the living room of my house and my parents and siblings could see me. It was normal to them, so they didn't mind. If I was at my grandparent's house, I would do it out in the open where they or anyone else who was there could see me. They also didn't care. I remember being babysat by my cousin Melissa and my aunt Debbie and doing my rope out in the open when I was with them as well. When I was very little, before I had figured out a way to do it in my head, I used to do my rope at my brothers' football games. Football days were very long days. My brothers were not on the same team, which made the day even longer because I had to sit through multiple football games. All the while, if I could not do my rope, I would most definitely have a meltdown. In those instances, strangers or other football families saw me do my rope. I vividly remember doing my rope behind the bleachers at one of their games and having a little boy look at me. He was walking by and his mom was holding his hand. I remember her kind of turning him the other way and trying to get him not to look at me. I was very, very little when that happened and I remember it well. I think I remember it because it was my first inclination my rope was not normal to other people. It was not something everyone did and, of course, as an egocentric child, I didn't understand that. But it was something *I* did. I hadn't yet developed any type of insecurities to make me worried about what other people thought of my rope.

Now, my rope is confined to my room and nobody sees it. I only make my noise if it is strictly my parents and siblings in the house. They are the only ones that ever hear me do my rope through the walls. If there is someone else in the house, I will not make my humming noise. The sound, just like the physical motion, definitely enhances my experience, but I can sacrifice it for awhile if someone is over. My brother-in-law Teddy has just barely passed the test after thirteen years of being with my sister. He also used to see me do my rope out in the open when I was little, but it became different for me once I got older and I started to develop insecurities regarding my rope. When I am on vacation, I will shut myself up in the bathroom and my family has to knock very gingerly if they need to come in. Except for my dad. He just throws open the door without a care in the world. My brother Austin will also throw open the door, but step to the side, so that I know he doesn't see me. Every year, most of my extended family goes on vacation at the beach together and we all stay in the same hotel. My parents and siblings will go outside on the deck for an hour (or more if that is what I need) so that I can do my rope in private. I have a very, very supportive and accepting family. That is what someone like me needs more than anything. A supportive and accepting family. I remember once asking Lindsey how they did it. I have put her and Teddy out many times late at night when they come home to visit. They always get my room when they are here and they sacrifice going to bed so that I can do my rope for a few extra minutes. (I'm a night owl). I remember asking her, "How do you do it? How do you all of you guys put up with me making my noise and not being able to go in the room while I am in there?" And she said to me, "When you love the person, you don't mind." That is really all I could ever ask for.

Chapter Three: Walking in Squares

Emotions often drive the behaviors in good ways and bad.

   Along with my rope, I also have something that I call my music. This one has its name for a little bit more obvious reasons. It involves listening to music. It has gone through many phases as well and it is still evolving in a lot of ways. The purpose of my music is also to stim, but I stim with it in a different way. When I listen to music, I HAVE to be moving. There is no doing my music in my head. Both my rope and my music involve a lot of physical activity and whenever I feel excited or happy, the first thing I want to do is my music. Doing my music helps me sort out and process new information in my head, which is very similar to what my rope does, but my music involves my emotions. My own feelings of excitement, happiness, sadness, or anger are present when I do my music, and it helps me to regulate them.

   My music came into my life a little bit later than my rope did. I was very early into elementary school when I started to love music, and I was able to use it in this way. Before I discovered the music aspect, I was able to stim through different forms of physical activity. Running, jumping, swinging, swimming, or riding carnival rides were all ways that I have been able to stim my entire life without needing the music. The physical activity is the main part of the stim and the music just adds to it. When I started going to school, I used to blare music through my stereo in my bedroom. I was about five years old at the time and my brothers always tell me of their mornings when they were in middle school where they were woken up by Hannah Montana and High School Musical songs every single day. I used to do my music bright and early so I was refreshed by the time I left for school that day. I actually still do it that way and usually, if I can't do my music before I leave the house for some reason, I will have a pretty hard day just because I will be a little more agitated than usual. However, I now use my headphones so as not to disturb everybody. My music is just as essential to me as my rope. I need to do it every single day and the feeling only gets worse if I don't. When I do my music in my room, I am simultaneously pacing while I listen. When I would blare my music in my room when I was little, I would walk in squares. That is actually what my music used to be referred to as by my family: walking in squares. My room has always had to be organized in a specific way to give me enough room to do this. Everything had to be pushed up against the walls to give me my main walking space. I still set up my room with this in mind. I don't know why walking in squares is what I used to like to do, but it kind of evolved into just simple pacing. I needed the physical activity, but the music gave me a rhythm to move to. Pacing is basically all I can do in my room because I have a limited amount of space to move.

After awhile, I got what I used to call my "listener." It was a little portable music player with pretty pink and purple flowers on it that I could put my CD in and listen to music while I was out other places. My older brothers were always involved in sports year round, and I would take my listener with me to every football, basketball, and baseball event. Just like my rope, I was a little bit too embarrassed to do it in public once I got to be a certain age. Like I said, I used to do my rope right out where everyone could see me, but once I got a little bit older, I knew these behaviors were odd to other people and they didn't know what they meant or why I did them. I would rather just blend in than draw attention to myself like that, so I devised a plan to be able to do my music without the physical activity, just like I can do my rope without physically using my rope. I tied the two of them together. I did say there is no doing my music in my head and that is the truth. However, I realized I could do both my rope and my music at the same time in my mind. I could listen to my music and hear the lyrics of the songs, and I could put those words onto the pictures in my mind. It was perfect and I have done it like that ever since. I, of course, still do both of them separately when I am in private but, in a situation where I need to release those feelings while I am out in public, I can do it this way if I have music available. This actually gives me more satisfaction in terms of my rope than it does my music (because they both give me fulfillment in different ways), but it is the way I can incorporate my music into my rope. I usually always carry my IPod or my phone with me, and if I have either of those things, I almost always have a pair of headphones with me as well. When I am at the store, for example, I can put one headphone in and turn on some music on low volume if I get the feeling that I need to stim. It doesn't have the same effect without the physical activity, but it will work for the time being. Having the music playing in one ear softly can help me to get through the day just as doing my rope in my head can help me get through the day.

After a few years of doing my music, I discovered a new physical activity I loved that worked with it. When I was eleven years old, I learned to ride my bike without training wheels. I was pretty delayed in this area. I am not a very coordinated person by ANY means, and I have never had very good balancing skills, especially when I was younger. I have also always lived my life afraid of doing anything that could hurt me, and I knew if I tried to ride a bike, I would most likely get hurt. Thus, an eleven year old with training wheels I was. The summer before I went into fifth grade, my family was on our annual beach vacation and there was a bike path right in front of our hotel. Every year, we go on bike rides together on the bike path, and even though I was the only one with training wheels, I would still go on the bike ride with all of my cousins. The training wheels made a huge amount of noise when I rode along that bumpy path and people stared, of course. This particular summer, my family had been hard pressed on getting me to learn without training wheels. I was not too keen on the idea. It wasn't that I didn't want to learn; I was just afraid and I almost felt defeated. I knew I couldn't do it. Lindsey and Teddy rented me a bike when we were at the beach and they all tried to help me learn. My cousin Maddie got on it and said, "Look, Jill. It's really easy!" Only a couple seconds later, she accidentally rode right off the bike path screaming, and it only confirmed that I wasn't ready for that yet. We were riding our bikes along the bike path a little while later when I got passed up by a boy about four years old on his bike that did not have training wheels. After that, I was determined to learn how to ride without training wheels.

About a week later after we returned home, I was riding my bike without training wheels and FAST. On our property, we have a very long driveway and when you turn into our house, you have to come down a small incline. After I learned to ride my bike, I rode in really fast figure-eights up and down the driveway constantly. By then, I had an iPod with all of my favorite songs on it, and I was able to clip that to my shirt while I rode. It was something I loved doing and I did it for hours every day all through middle school and even into high school. Anyone who lived anywhere near my house probably saw me on my bike 95% of the times they drove by. When I was a freshman, my brother Austin told me a story about a guy he had met at one of his co-ed softball games. He had seen me ride my bike in figure-eights every time he drove by and he asked Austin if I happened to be on the autism spectrum. Of course, he told him that I was indeed on the autism spectrum, and when he told me about this conversation, I was honored. I was in a stage where I was feeling a little bit more comfortable with who I was and it made me feel good that somebody paid enough attention to notice that about me.

Occasionally, my brothers took me on big bike rides around the countryside near where we live and that was a lot of fun. But I never wanted to ride slower to stay with them; I just wanted to listen to my music and go. However, I couldn't do that and they knew it so they kept a close eye on me. They sometimes would let me ride a little bit ahead for a few seconds and then they would yell behind me telling me to stop and wait for them. When I am doing my music like that, it can be dangerous. My mind goes to other places. When I have the physical activity portion of my music, I'm not paying attention to the lyrics and I'm not thinking about the pictures in my brain. If I am doing my rope and my music together, that is what I am doing. But when it is just my music, the things that are going on in my head are totally different. Instead, I am imagining myself in other places. My emotions are very vivid in these moments, and I am not generally seeing or thinking about what is going on around me. I wouldn't know if there was a car coming up behind me or if there was a person following me. Therefore, I have to be very careful when I am doing things like this because something could happen pretty easily.

When I got to high school, I was allowed to go off campus for lunch. My freshman and sophomore years, I would walk with my friends to the nearby grocery store or to the bowling alley that was just down the road from my school. When I would do that, I liked to put one headphone in and listen to music while I walked. It was a nice little window of time where I had the opportunity to stim during the school day. However, after my parents found out I was doing that, they didn't really want me to do it anymore. They were worried about cars and strangers because, even with a group of girls at lunch laughing and talking to each other, I was not present in the moment. When I am doing my music, I am off somewhere else in my mind, and I am not always aware of what is happening right in front of my face. My mom and Austin even pulled into the driveway when I was out there once and just waited in the car for me to notice they were there and move out of the way. There have been times where things have snapped me out of it, such as one of my dogs barking or suddenly being right next to my feet when I turn around. But when I have my headphones on while listening to music, it makes it even harder to notice things like that or be alerted by them. I can't hear a lot of the outside noises along with the fact that my mind isn't present there.

In my mind while I am doing my music, I am thinking of different scenarios and I imagine myself in them. Some of them are real scenarios I have actually lived through and some of them are made up. Typically, they mirror the reality of my day or the emotions I have been feeling. It is a great way that I can escape for a little while and when I am done, I usually feel ready to conquer the rest of the day. That is because I am able to sort out what I am feeling and process through all of my thoughts that can be pretty overwhelming a lot of the time. I can do this by putting myself in the shoes of another person in my mind, or I imagine myself doing things I wish I could do. I will think about people I came across that day and try to see myself through their eyes. I imagine myself filling a role I really want to fill or saying things I really want to say. I might even imagine myself being friends with someone I wish I could be friends with. (Like in fifth grade, I imagined myself as Justin Bieber's girlfriend, of course!) It is kind of like I am living a different life in my mind. I often compare it to watching a movie or a show on television. That is essentially what I am doing, except I am making it all up as I go and I am the only one who can see it.

When I have big things coming up in my life, I imagine what they will be like in my head through my music, and it can actually prepare me for it. However, when I was younger, it used to give me false hope. For example, I would imagine myself going to a party and being able to talk to everybody there effortlessly and, of course, that would never really happen. In those situations, I would let myself down in real life because I had imagined things going such a different way than they actually did. In some ways, I imagine myself living a life free of some of the things that are part of my autism and that is not always a great thing either because I have autism and I always will. I don't wish I didn't have autism. I know my autism is a part of who I am as a person and I would never want to change that. But when I do my music, I will usually see myself not having some of the troubles I have due to being autistic. I am a little bit better now at being able to separate my music world from my real life and remember that they are not the same thing. I might still feel disappointed when things don't go the way I expected them to, but I don't put so much emphasis on things going the exact way I pictured them going in my music world.

My emotions play a big role in my music, and the scenarios I think up are typically based on the emotions I am really feeling. On a day where I am feeling exceptionally down about my situation, maybe I had a meltdown that day or I am really anxious about something, what I imagine will reflect those thoughts. The scenario will be anxious or sad. And the songs I choose to listen to will be as well. I will imagine that morbid or depressing things are happening to me and because my emotions are so connected to me when I do my music, I will physically bawl my eyes out about something that didn't even really happen. I am actually crying because something happened that really bothered me and when I do my music, I am processing through those negative emotions I have been feeling. By doing this, I am able to release them by putting myself in a different place, a different scenario, a different world set aside from the one I am actually in. There have been times where maybe I got my feelings hurt at school that day, and I have been pretty down in the dumps ever since. When it gets to be night time and I am in my room alone doing my music, I am able to finally release those feelings of sadness and hurt by imagining a different scenario aside from the one I am actually facing. Of course, there are times when I am very upset in the moment, and I cry about the things that are actually bothering me, but there are a lot of times where I feel the need to cry and I almost can't until I let myself through my music. On the contrary, when I am in a good mood, I will imagine myself doing fun or exciting things, and the songs I listen to will be more upbeat and happy. My emotions are connected in this way also. To use my example again, if I imagine I am at a party, and I can talk to everyone effortlessly, I actually feel the freeing feeling that would come with that. Going to a party and talking to everyone there effortlessly? That is my dream! When I am able to think about that through doing my music, I feel elated and not trapped in a mind full of anxieties, which happens to be the reality of my life. I am putting myself in a different place, and it is a way that I can process through the emotions I am feeling right at that very moment.

When I hear about something that makes me excited, I feel like I have to do my music. The feeling just comes right in and hits me full force. When I found out my sister was engaged, or when I got student of the month in high school, the excitement I feel gives me the urge to move. This is another way that my emotions get connected to the physical activity. My music is made up of quite a few things: music, physical activity, emotions, and imagination. Doing something like walking in squares or riding my bike while I have my headphones on is when my emotions and my imagination are at their peak. All of it together is the way I stim.

The summer going into my seventh grade year, we were on our annual beach trip and my uncle Larry Howard had noticed that my tires on my bike were worn almost completely thin. I had ridden it so much that they no longer had any tread on them. My grandpa had started to store extra tools in the garage for when I would get a flat tire or just needed a bike repair because it happened all the time. I have always lived at a frenetic pace. I am pretty much constantly moving all day long. I will go from one thing to the next. I'll be doing my rope, get the urge to run, come inside and write, and go run again. My freshman year, my brother Ethan put his Fit Bit on my wrist from eleven o'clock in the morning to two o'clock in the afternoon and, by just doing all of the things

I normally do, I had walked five and a half miles. I am constantly moving. I rode my bike constantly, and whenever something happened that got in the way of riding, it really bothered me. A few weeks after our beach trip, the chain on my bike was broken. I had just gotten new tires so I was all fixed up and ready to go until this happened. There were people over so I didn't have anyone available to fix it for me. My cousin Remy and I decided to take it upon ourselves to fix the chain, and then I carried out the really smart act of riding my bike down the incline first thing. Of course, we actually didn't know how to fix the chain, so it broke again on my way down the hill. I flew off my seat and practically over my handle bars and scraped myself up on the asphalt pretty bad. After that, I incorporated a lot more running in the driveway into my daily routine instead of riding my bike. Now, all I do is run.

When I am at home and I have a strong feeling, no matter what it is, I jump up, I go outside, and I run. I run back and forth sometimes for an hour at a time. When it is dark out, I am in my room pacing. I used to like to run in my driveway at night too, but my mom put an end to that because, like I said before, I am not aware of what is happening around me. The first thing I do when I get home from work or school is put my headphones in and run in the driveway. It is the first thing I do when I get up in the morning. I jump out of bed, get dressed, and I'm out the door. I also tend to pace a lot while I am out in the driveway, but I mostly run. I will sporadically get the need to run throughout the day. All through high school, I used to get the mail for our house and my grandparents' house. Our mailboxes are at the end of our driveway and I would run and get my parents' mail, run it to our house, and leave it on the counter. Then I would run back to the mailbox, get the mail for my grandparents, run it to their house, and then run back home all while I had music blaring in my ears. That was part of my routine all through high school. And I never took the time to change my shoes. If I had on Converse, I ran to the mailbox and back in Converse. If I had on boots, I ran in boots. Now I understand a little bit better that I could ruin my feet by doing this, so I try to force myself to take the time to change my shoes before I run. My music isn't as private as my rope is. People that drive by my house do see me do it, even though they don't actually know what I'm doing. However, my really emotional part of my music is a lot more private. When I am outside running, I am not typically letting out my emotions right there in the open. I am definitely still thinking about the scenarios in my mind and imagining myself in other places, but I usually save my really emotional moments for when I am in my bedroom at night by myself.

To summarize, my emotions basically cause me to feel the need to do my music. Even when I am not necessarily happy or sad, I still have to do my music every day. However, if I have a strong feeling of emotions at any point, the need to do it gets stronger and I will usually do my music for a longer period of time in that case. It can be done through running, pacing back and forth in my room, or riding in a car. Just sitting and listening to music has no effect on me whatsoever. I have to be moving. I like to take advantage of any type of car ride where I am not the one driving to do my music. I put my headphones in so I can have the songs I prefer (which are all different kinds of genres and artists), and I listen while I ride. If I am riding in a car and we are at a stop light, I will usually pause the song. When the light turns green and the car starts moving again, I will unpause it. Though I am technically just sitting in the car, the movement of the vehicle is enough that it works. I need the physical part of it, but if I can't do it physically, doing it with my rope (putting the words on the pictures) in my head will suffice.

Basically, I never just listen to music. I listen to music while either processing my emotions, imagining myself in other places, or putting words onto pictures and always, always moving. If I am not moving, I am wishing that I was moving. I am deathly afraid of ever getting injured in a way that would make it so I was confined for any period of time and unable to move the way I need to. When I get sick, it is torture. There have been times where I was sick and I didn't care. I still had to get my stimming in for the day and by doing so, I would just make myself a lot more sick. One time when I was very sick, I did it to the point where I hallucinated and passed out. It is difficult to not be able to do my rope and my music in those times, but typically, I can turn on the T.V. and put the words on the pictures in my head. I always have that never-ending sea of pictures in there for whenever I might need them, which is every day without fail.

By doing my rope and my music, I am able to decompress and cope with the things going on in my life. There was a morning a few weeks ago where I was nervous about something happening with school and I was crying. I didn't have class until that afternoon and my parents were at work, so I was home alone. My dad called me on the phone from work to ask me what my plans were for the day because he knew I was nervous. I told him what was bothering me and I think he was surprised at how upset I sounded. He promptly said, "Okay. Go do your rope and your music and calm down." They are both a way for me to gather my thoughts and my emotions, and I always feel better after doing them. They are my biggest coping mechanism. Just having a few minutes to do my rope and my music can change the entire outcome of my day. I need a little bit of time to myself to decompress and gather my thoughts and then I am ready to go. When I am feeling stressed, the feeling to do my rope and my music gets even stronger, so it is important that I am able to work that time in so I don't fall apart at the stress of it all.

Chapter Four: Elephant Alphabet

Some things that are easy for you are hard for us and things that are easy for us are hard for you.

When I was little, I used to memorize movies. When I would do my rope in front of the T.V., I was able to memorize the entire movie word for word. When I got a little bit older, I used to memorize certain episodes of shows I would watch on Disney Channel. I remember when I was in second grade, I was on my way to the Mind Institute in Sacramento for an evaluation. They were doing a study on autism in girls, and I was one of their subjects. I spent a half hour reciting an entire Hannah Montana episode to my parents and grandparents during the car ride. Doing this didn't really mean anything to me. I picked up on the fact that people thought it was neat so I loved to show it off. But as for the actual memorization, it was a piece of cake. It didn't take hardly any work other than doing my rope, but that was something I loved doing. Repeating the words in my mind was also something I loved doing. I have always had a fascination with words and names. I like certain sounds and I like to say them. When I was little, I used to repeat certain words over and over again because I liked the sound of them and I wanted to say them. There were also certain sounds I loved to hear, such as a car door closing, and I would open and shut the car door multiple times just to hear that sound.

Since I put words on pictures when I do my rope either physically or in my head, I can sometimes think back on the pictures and remember what was said. Also, I think the analyzation of the words as they are being spoken is the reason for my memorization as well. When I have any type of social interaction, I will go over it in my head repeatedly afterwards. I can almost always tell you exactly what I said and exactly what the other person said because I am analyzing it so much. After I walk away, I will think about how the person smiled (or didn't), what they might have thought about what I said, or even what they may have meant by certain things. A lot of times, I won't even realize someone was being rude or sarcastic until I think about the interaction I had with that person later. I will also realize mistakes I made in the conversation I hadn't originally noticed I was making. My constant over-analyzation of everything that happens to me socially can sometimes be a burden I can't help but bear. I can't turn my brain off, and though I do want to think about those things so I know where I can improve socially, it also has a tendency to make me feel like I am totally socially inept, which actually isn't true at all. I'm not bound by a social deficit that stems from my disability. I have had to work harder at it than others and it doesn't come naturally to me, but I have made a lot of positive strides in that area over the last couple of years.

Just like I analyze social interactions in my real day-to-day life, I also analyze them when I watch movies or T.V. shows. I have always loved watching reality television in particular and I think there are two reasons for it. I like that they are real people doing real things. I used to be terrified of animated movies when I was little, and I never wanted to watch them. I think that is partly because I couldn't comprehend the fact it wasn't real and it just scared me. Most classic Disney movies that everyone knows like the back of their hand, I have never even seen because I hated the animation. I watched the new edition of The Lion King for the first time a few weeks ago, and I think I was probably the only person at that theater who didn't know what was going to happen next. The animation was just too much for me to process when I was a little girl. Therefore, watching real people do realistic things makes a lot more sense to me. But I also like to watch reality television because I can analyze the social interaction between the people I watch. I have always kind of used it as a way to practice understanding social cues and mistakes.Typically, whenever I watch T.V., I am doing my rope in my head. When I do this, I am usually sitting down, whether it be at home or in class. Sitting for long periods of time can be hard for me. I like to be up and moving. Usually, if I am confined to a chair (like when I am in class for long periods of time), I will do my rope in my head to pass the time. It relaxes me and it makes it possible for me to make it through that time where I have to be sitting. That is also the reason I did it when I was little, and that is why I memorized the movies when nobody even knew I was doing that. I didn't even realize I was doing that while I was doing it. I was just doing my rope in my head, like I always did, but when I would think of the movie later, I eventually realized I was able to literally go through it in my head word for word.

At the age I am today, I am still able to memorize movies and T.V. shows by doing my rope in my head. I will sometimes see a movie I really enjoyed watching and I will want to watch it over and over again. A couple of years ago, I had a favorite Thanksgiving themed Hallmark movie on DVD and I loved the storyline of it. It wasn't exactly a realistic plot, but I loved the words and the setting and just everything about the movie. I had it playing one morning when Lindsey and Teddy were home for Thanksgiving, and it was just running in the background of our conversations. Throughout the day, whenever it ended, I would just start it back over and watch bits and pieces of it. Later that night, we were playing board games, which is our late-night ritual every time they come home to visit, and Teddy said, "Is this the same movie that was on this morning?" Without even looking, I just said, "Yup." A couple of days later, I could recite that movie word for word, if you had asked me to. I could have told you their names, what happened next at any given part, and the sequence of events that led up to the all-too-happy ending. I could have told you the date the main character marked on her calendar at the beginning of the movie was November 3rd, which is my brother Austin's birthday. It is also my little cousin Benedict's birthday, Kendall Jenner's birthday, and one of my teacher friends, Mrs. Bishop's, wedding anniversary. I could have told you the main character's last names, which changed throughout the movie, matched up to all of the things she was fighting to protect (she was a lawyer). I noticed the little things and the big things. I paid attention to the small details, and I memorized the entire movie. I also used to love the Narnia movies when I was little and my mind basically became Narnia. I mirrored those movies in my own life. I recited lines from them all the time. I became obsessed with swords and bow and arrows, and I perfected my British accent. It is a long-standing joke in my family to yell out the words, "Beavers don't talk!" in a British accent because I always yelled that out when I was little due to that being my favorite line in the movie.

My memorization did not stop at just movies. I have been a memorizing machine for as long as I can remember. It is probably the greatest strength I possess. When I was two, I could say the alphabet backwards. I still can. Over the years, I have perfected it into the same sing-songy tune of the actual ABC's. Z,Y,X,W,V,U,T. S,R,Q,P,O,N,M. L,K,J,I,H,G,F. E,D,C,B,A. I learned how to do it when I spent all of those hours with Grandma Howard in the pink bedroom. She had an alphabet puzzle that, when put together, was a picture of an elephant. Each piece had a different letter on it and the pieces were different colors. I used to dump them out on the floor near her recliner and sort them into groups of red, purple, yellow, and green. Then, I would carefully place all of the reds on the puzzle in their collective spots throughout the alphabet, then the yellows, then the purples, and then the greens. I would switch up the order I put them on. Sometimes I would sort them by shape instead of color. Some of the pieces had a more ragged edge while others were perfect squares. Sometimes I would put all of the exterior pieces on and then fill in the middle pieces. I had all sorts of different rituals I would go through to put it together, and it was my favorite thing to work on. When I was that age, my mom was the youth group leader at the church we attended in town. I used to take my toys and my rope and watch as Ethan and Austin played games with all of their friends and my mom gave Christ-centered lessons. One evening, mostly everyone had left, but my mom was still having a conversation with another lady from church. I was standing outside the door listening to their conversation, and I could hear this woman telling my mom about someone she knew who could say the alphabet backwards. It was as if a lightbulb went off in my head, and I came to the realization that *I* could say the alphabet backwards. I searched through my mind for a picture of the elephant puzzle in Grandma Howard's room, and when I had it vivid in my brain, I marched in there and said, "I can do that," and I did. I was two and my mom has never forgotten it.

Today, I memorize dates and names the best. I know the birthdays of people who probably don't even know my name. I know most of the birthdays of the people I went to school with, almost all of my family members, a ton of celebrities, and pretty much anyone I deem important in my life. Anyone I have ever been friends with on Facebook can almost guarantee I know their birthday, unless I haven't heard it before. All I need to do is hear it once and then it is forever engraved in my brain. I know what day an important event happened, I know anniversaries, and I KNOW names. Names are one of my favorite topics of conversation. I like to say things like, "I think this name is pretty," "I only like this name when it is spelled this way," or "What kind of a name is that?" I wish I could have about twenty-five daughters because that is how many girl names I have picked out. I just LOVE names. As far as dates go, I could be asked about pretty much any date on the calendar, and I can tell you something that happened on that day. Every morning when I wake up, I go through this ritual in my mind. I think about what date it is, and then I go through the birthdays and/or other important events that are significant to that day.

I have a very clear picture of each month and day in my head. It is in the formation of the letter Z. I can say the same for the regular alphabet and the numbers one through one hundred. In terms of the months, it goes straight across from January to May, and then those summer months slant down diagonally, just like the letter Z does, and then September to December are straight across as well. My picture in my head of my numbers makes a backwards Z formation. It goes straight across from one to twenty, diagonally all the way up until eighty-nine, and then it goes straight across from ninety to one hundred. When I am counting, I am seeing this picture in my mind as if it were right there in front of me. If I were to count higher, it would do the same for every set of one hundred numbers. The way I see the alphabet is not in the form of a Z, however, it is broken into four straight lines, which are the exact same lines as Grandma Howard's elephant puzzle. That is how I learned it and so that is how I see it. For the months of the year, I can narrow it down and picture a specific month, and then I will have a clear picture of each of the dates in that month in my head as well. Typically, they are separated by approximately ten days at a time so I will see, for example, the first of January through the tenth. Then, below it will be the eleventh through the twentieth and then below that is the twenty-first through the thirty-first. This is something I can actually see in my mind, and almost every day on the calendar has at least one person or event on it.

     I can be asked about that specific date and I will picture my yearly calendar Z formation, then I will picture the specific month, then the specific line (out of the three groups of ten) the particular date would be on, and then, finally, I will picture the specific date. When I explain this, it makes it sound like a long process that would take me awhile to get through, but it actually only spans a couple of seconds. When I learn someone's birthday, I will put them on that date in my mind very similarly to how I put the words onto the pictures. There are some dates on the calendar I don't have anything or anybody on just because I haven't ever had anything to put on that particular date. However, the majority of all dates have at least something on them in my mind. In other words, when I said that November 3rd is my brother Austin, my baby cousin Benedict, and Kendall Jenner's birthday, that means I have them all pictured on that day. The same is said for Mrs. Bishop's anniversary on that day as well. The pictures in this way are different from the pictures I use to do my rope. Typically, I picture the people doing whatever I last saw them doing or the last picture I saw of them. To keep using the example of November 3rd, the last thing I saw my brother Austin doing was playing bean bag toss at our family Easter party. When I think of him, I will actually be able to picture him doing that in my mind. For Mrs. Bishop's anniversary, I will be able to see the pictures I have actually seen of her on her wedding day. Because I am able to picture people doing things the way I saw them doing, it is easy for me to be able to remember people's mannerisms and characteristics. I am pretty good at knowing how certain people walk, talk, smile, and laugh, and I can usually imitate people pretty well because of this.

     I used to have Ethan and Austin's high school yearbooks memorized in alphabetical order. They were two years apart in school, so there were quite a few times where they had the same yearbook.

They had two separate books, but they had all of the same exact content in them. When Austin was a freshman and Ethan was a junior, I was in third grade, and that was the first year I memorized their yearbooks. I had some sort of obsession with yearbooks when I was younger. I think it was probably the fact that there was an abundance of pictures to memorize, and then put words on when I did my rope, which is exactly what I did. At the end of the school year, I would steal them from my brothers and do my rope to all of the pictures. I eventually knew all of the names and faces of their classmates, and I knew which background color every individual person had in their school picture. I had the pictures stored away in my brain where a lot of them still are. I paid particular attention to the grades the boys were in. I probably could have lined up the classes of 2010 and 2012 in alphabetical order if I had tried, and I would have been able to tell you the color shirt that people had been wearing when they got their pictures taken.

At the end of Austin's sophomore year and Ethan's senior year, I was looking at Austin's yearbook (I drew on people's faces in Ethan's once and thus I was banned) and the previous year was the first time I had really memorized his grade. I skimmed over the pictures of the sophomores and I said, "Austin, where did he go?" He said, "Who?" I told him the name of the person I was referring to and I said, "He is gone. He used to be in between these two people in alphabetical order. Did he move?" Austin was confused at how I knew that a person was missing but, upon further inspection, I found several more people who indeed did not have pictures who definitely had pictures in the yearbook the previous year. I also saw new people had been added. I was able to notice this because I had the order already memorized in my head from the previous year and it wasn't matching up. Some people were missing and some people were new. The next two years of his high school career, this became like a game to me. His junior year, I looked and found new people or people who were missing and did the same for his senior year. Even now, I still know pretty much every single person that was in his and Ethan's graduating class by name. I haven't looked at their pictures in a long time and I don't really remember the order they were in, but I definitely know them. There have been times where I have been with Ethan and Austin out at the store or something and I'll say, "Didn't you go to school with that guy?" They'll say, "I don't know." And I'll just reply, "Are you kidding me? You did!" Just a few weeks ago, my mom and I were taking my dad lunch at work, and we saw someone who she thought looked familiar. I said, "Yeah, that's because he went to school with Ethan. His name is Devan." When I finished my sixth grade year, I got my very own yearbook with pictures of people I went to school with and I was so excited. I memorized the pictures just like I did with my brothers'. All of the background colors were the same gray, but I can still picture in my head all of the faces of the kids who were in eighth grade that year. I went over that year the most because their pictures were bigger, and they came first in the yearbook. Eventually, I fell out of that yearbook obsession, but I definitely still remember a lot of names and faces because of it.

When I memorize things, I get a lot of fulfillment. For me, it is not a very difficult thing to do and it involves my rope, which is what I love. In terms of pictures, it gives me more of a variety when I do my rope, and it can be a coping mechanism for me as well. There have been times where I was extremely anxious or upset or disappointed, and without even realizing it, I will slowly be going over the thousands of pictures in my mind. It is kind of like a museum of pictures right there in my head, and it serves a lot of purpose for me. A few years ago, I watched parts of the Temple Grandin movie. I only watched parts of it because a lot of that movie was too real for me and it was uncomfortable for me to watch it. But there is a specific thing they incorporated into that movie that really resonated with me because I knew exactly what it meant. All of the times where the actor who plays Temple Grandin is staring at the wall or other objects, and she is drawing pictures in her mind, are all times where I knew what she was doing because I do that too. Just like I said that I go through my pictures when I get upset, I also put pictures on the wall or the fireplace or whatever I am staring at in that moment. The fact that the visual of that is in the movie is really meaningful and it makes me realize things I don't even know that I am doing, things that just seem like ordinary things going on in my mind, are actually autistic things. I wouldn't have ever known it without seeing some of that movie. Now I know that part of the memorizing pictures and looking through them in my head when I am upset is something other people do too.

Chapter Five: Flower Patch

What you see is not what you get. There is so much more than what meets the eye.

Before all of this came to be, I was a baby. I was born in the late summer of 1999 to my parents Joe and Elaine Schmeltzer. I was their fourth child born after my older sister, Lindsey, and my older brothers, Ethan and Austin. When I was born, Lindsey was twelve, Ethan was eight, and Austin was six. I have lived in the same house in the same small town in Northern California my whole life. I am the youngest of eight grandkids on my mom's side, and I grew up living right next door to my grandparents. My Aunt Julie, my Uncle John, and two of my cousins, Natalie and Blake, lived on the other end of the property. My other two first cousins on my mom's side, Remy and Rebecca, lived in Southern California and they, along with my aunt and uncle, Ron and Robin, came up to visit for six weeks during the summer and two weeks at Christmas. My great-grandmother (my Grandma Howard) had five children and my grandma was right in the middle. From those five children came eleven grandchildren, twenty-seven great-grandchildren, and thirteen great-great-grandchildren so far. These people have all made up the family parties and gatherings I have experienced for every holiday throughout my entire life, and our roots are firmly planted here with generations that came before us. On my dad's side of the family, I am the second to the youngest grandchild out of thirty-one total grandchildren. As of now, there are forty-one total great-grandchildren. My dad grew up in Wyoming with his eight siblings, Janet, Margaret, Phil, Tom, Nancy, John, Fran, and Chris, and the majority of his family still lives there. I was immediately anchored in a lot of family traditions and values when I came into the world and I still hold true to those today. Having grown up with lots of family members around me all the time, I was used to having a lot of things happening and a large family was normal to me.

During my first year of life, my mom had a lot of concerns about me. Since I was her fourth baby, she noticed differences in me that weren't present with her older three children at that age. I was lucky my mom had three children before me, while also having two boys and two girls, because it made her notice there was something different about me. I wasn't just doing certain things because I was a girl and girls and boys are different. She had seen what having children without autism was like and now she had me. She didn't know at the time that I was autistic, but she knew I was different. She spent many years trying to get everyone else to see it too. This could seem like the opposite of what most people would do. When I was little, she was told by her friends or anyone else she was talking to that their children also did those same things I was doing. I think most people probably thought they were making her feel better by saying that, but it kind of has the opposite effect on mothers like her. She was feeling only the beginning of the misunderstandings that were inevitably going to happen, even when I was that little.

It is the same feeling I often feel now as a young adult with autism and that I definitely felt as an autistic teenager. It is easy to look at me and think that I am experiencing things that everyone experiences, such as anxiety, and sum it up to just that. Why should I get that "special treatment" in school if I am dealing with something that everyone deals with in their life? But the reason is the not-so-simple fact that it is very different. It is a different kind of anxiety. It is a lot like what other people experience, but it is a whole lot different too. Everyone else does not have a different wiring in their brain. Not everyone has those neurological differences. Everyone is not autistic. Maybe I am feeling the same thing everyone else feels from time to time, but not everyone has something like a rope that they need to get them through the day and not everyone has a communication deficit the way I do. Autism is different in everyone it affects. That statement is true. But a lot of us struggle in the same ways.

Some of us aren't obviously different and others of us are a bit more noticeably different. It is a very broad spectrum and there are people experiencing every inch of it. There are some people who didn't get diagnosed until they were well into adulthood, and they didn't get those services they might have needed as a child. Some adults still don't have an official diagnosis and they are self-diagnosed as autistic. Some people are unable to communicate vocally. Some people can talk very well. Some people have a really difficult time functioning in the world, and they need their "rope world" to cope with the stresses of it all, while others don't have a brain that requires as much stimulation. Some people look like nothing is wrong when really they are trying very hard to keep themselves together. And some people are unable to keep themselves together, but we are all human beings on this planet. We all have feelings and we all have underlying struggles within ourselves that you can't see. We all have minds that work in similar ways. Just because you can't always see it doesn't mean it isn't there and doesn't mean it doesn't have anything to bring to this world. Some autistic people feel like they are aliens living on a planet that they don't belong on where nobody understands them or speaks their language. I get that. I have had points in my life where I have definitely felt that way. Just because you can't physically see that I have a disability does not mean my struggles are not real. I am able to function better than some and I can use my voice more than others. But it is still hard to be a part of this society, and every single one of us is struggling in our own unique ways. For everyone around us, it is only a matter of being mindful of it and being willing to see it. That is the first step.

The talk of what causes autism can be very controversial. Just like everyone is unique in their quirks and their struggles, they are unique in this way. Everyone who has autism started to show signs in different ways and at different times. Maybe it was when they first went to school and were around other children for the first time. Maybe it was when they did quirky little things as a toddler. Maybe it wasn't until they did their own research later in life and decided to get evaluated themselves. It is also dependent upon the people around them. If their parents know a lot about autism, they might notice it sooner. If they have never been around someone with autism, they might not notice it for a long time. Sometimes it might not even necessarily be the parents who initially notice it. In some cases, it may even go unnoticed forever. If people have only ever thought of an autistic person as someone who could not speak, then that thought might not even cross their minds. Sometimes it seems to be genetic and it is present in a lot of people in one family. Other times, it just kind of seems like it pops up out of nowhere.

There are a lot of factors that go into how autism is discovered in a person, and in my opinion, there are also a lot of factors that go into what causes autism in a person. If I was to make an educated guess, I would say there is more than one cause. I think that is the case because everyone has such a different story. I have had a few different theories about what caused my autism that I have pondered in the last few years. My mom had a miscarriage just a year before I was born. She has had thyroid problems throughout her life. She has an autoimmune disease. Because of these things, I often think that it could be something that has to do with hormones in the mother's body. But, of course, there are mothers of autistic children who have never had a miscarriage and there are mothers who have had miscarriages who do not have autistic children. There are mothers of autistic children without autoimmune diseases and thyroid issues, and there are mothers with those things who do not have autistic children. It really is a very mysterious thing and maybe we aren't supposed to know why it happens. If we knew, there might not be as many of us in the world. However, I do think, without hardly an inch of a doubt, that I was born with autism. I showed signs of autism as an infant and even as a newborn. For me, it has always been there. I am not a scientist or a doctor. I don't know what the case is for everyone else and I don't have any answers. But this is what happened to me.

The day of my birth was very eventful. It was Labor Day. My grandpa was on another floor of the hospital having a heart stent put in at the same time I was being born. I had a waiting room full of people there. My uncle even got a speeding ticket on the way to the hospital. There was a lot of anticipation and excitement. However, one of my brothers struggled with having my parents gone, so my dad could not spend the night at the hospital. Over the night, I had a few incidents where I choked and gagged and the nurses had to help me. The night I came home, I had what appeared to be a seizure. My dad flipped me over and my head was bobbing up and down while my eyes rolled back into my head. Even my siblings recall this moment very vividly and my sister has told me about how scary it was. My mom made a few phone calls and they had to stay up to keep a close eye on me. In the end, I was fine and those episodes never ended up being explained.

This was the start of a lot of unexplainable things I did as an infant, such as being very particular about the way I was fed. I didn't like to eat while I was being held and I didn't want to see the person feeding me. I usually wouldn't eat otherwise. I had lost nearly two pounds when my mom realized that I would eat with a bottle in these very specific ways. The pediatrician had referred my mom to a lactation specialist and she then went to my cousin Lori's house with my grandma. Lori is a nurse and she was helping my mom sterilize my bottles and feed me formula. They say I was way too thin, but after my mom had figured out the certain ways she could get me to eat, I was able to start gaining weight.

Over the course of the first few months of my life, I was a very quirky baby. I was extremely particular about everything that went on in my world and I was very high maintenance. I used to cry unexplainably all the time for what seemed like no reason at all. Looking back now, we all know it was probably sensory related. My grandma used to sit in her recliner for hours just to not wake me up until my mom got home. If I was being held, I refused to be facing inward. I wanted to be facing out with my back to the person holding me. I only tolerated a few people and I was very picky about who I would let hold me. On a trip to Wyoming during my first year, everyone was excited to see me and meet me for the first time. I was being passed around from person to person and my dad's dad, my Grandpa S. (short for Schmeltzer), yelled over top of everyone to hand me back to my mom and stop touching me. My mom has said I used to get so inconsolable when I was a baby that they used to have to leave places if someone I wasn't comfortable with picked me up. Even into my late childhood, there were certain events where this would happen. I used to be afraid of certain people in my family or at church who were loud and would do things that scared me, such as pick me up from behind when I wasn't expecting it. However, when I was a baby, it would have been more so obtaining to sensory issues/overstimulation I obviously couldn't explain because I was a baby.

I have had it held over my head my entire life by my older siblings that I never stopped crying. I can imagine there were a lot of sensory things that were already bothering me as a newborn and an infant. Maybe a certain piece of clothing or a certain noise would overstimulate me and that was the reason I cried so much. However, at the time, the reason for it was usually pretty unexplained and nobody could figure out exactly why I was crying. I just started and then didn't stop until I fell asleep. One morning, my mom was getting ready for work, and I was crying while sitting in a little carrier next to her in the bathroom. She started to blow dry her hair and I stopped crying. At first, it didn't register with her. She turned it off for a moment to do something else and I subsequently started to cry again. Then, when she started it back up again, she noticed that the crying stopped. After she realized the blow dryer was a way to soothe me, she took advantage of it and used it to do just that. She would turn it on and leave it running when I had gone into one of my crying spells and it worked. I would stop crying. Something about the noise just soothed me. She also used to run the vacuum to get me to stop crying and she would just stand it there and leave it running. My older siblings have also never let me live down the fact they couldn't hear the T.V. because the vacuum was constantly running. All of these were things my mom never had to worry about with Lindsey, Ethan, or Austin. I was a little bit different and she knew it even before my first birthday passed.

When I was a baby, my mom had a puzzle out on the floor. I was not even a year old and she said that I was able to put the puzzle together. She was amazed and she walked me down to my grandparents' house to show them what I could do. Not too long after that, we were on a trip to Wyoming to see my dad's side of the family. I had picked up a hair comb from somewhere in my grandparents' house and I was carrying it around with me. My mom was sitting at the table next to my Grandpa S. and I had the comb in my hands. I always had fly-away hair that stuck straight up on my head, so they were laughing at me. My mom asked me if I was going to comb my hair and my Grandpa

S. said to her, "Oh, she doesn't know what that means!" Right after he said that, I plopped the comb right onto my head, like I was going to start combing. Those are the kinds of stories my mom has always told me about ways she knew I was a little bit different. There is also a video of me at a year and a half singing the "Happy Birthday" song to Lindsey on her fourteenth birthday. I talked very early and was able to speak in full sentences by then. I was very observant and knew a lot about things going on in the world around me.

Though I don't remember any of these events and they are all just information given to me by my family, they all make sense to me. Given what I know now about my disability, I can see the signs all pointed in the direction of autism when I hear these stories. I know a lot of people don't want their children to struggle or be different. However, I don't like to think of autism as a bad thing. There are many autistic people who have a lot to offer to this world. Autism is just simply a different way of being and developing. Even though I know that to be true, I have had times where I wonder if my future children will inherit autism from me. I have always dreamed of being a mother, but it is something I am worried I will not be able to do. I inherited my mom's love of working with children. It runs deep in my blood. The majority of my family members are teachers, aspiring teachers, or retired teachers. We all love it, but I don't know if I will be able to handle having my own children one day.

First of all, my rope and my music are essential, as I have made very clear. They are a huge priority in my life and having to worry about taking care of a child on top of needing to do my rope and my music stresses me out. I can imagine that I wouldn't be able to do it as much, and that is a distressing thought for me. But I also worry about the inheritance of my struggles. What if I pass this down to my children, if I choose to have them later in life? It is an actual worry I have had for quite a few years. I know I will be able to be really understanding of a child in that situation, but I also know how difficult it can be, and I don't know how I would be able to experience both being on the spectrum and having a child on the spectrum. However, I know a lot about autism and I have my convictions. I don't think that I should be afraid of that. I think autism is a beautiful thing. It comes with its trials and its tribulations, but it is amazing. I wouldn't want to live my life any other way and I'm sure that the majority of autistic people would say the same thing if they were asked. There are times when I am absolutely angry that I have autism, but most of the time I am thankful I do. It is a different way of looking at the world that most people don't ever get the chance to see. In one of my papers I wrote in high school, I compared having autism to being like a flower. It needs a lot of love. It takes a lot of work. It requires a lot of being cared for and tended to. But, if you take care of it, if you show it love, if you put in the work, it blossoms. The storm clouds will come. The rain will fall. The thunder will roar. It may be the last one in the patch. But, eventually, the sun will shine and it will be beautiful. It just takes the extra work. When I see a child with the same autistic characteristics I had when I was their age, I think that there will need to be a lot of work put in and there is a lot of gardening to do. But there will come a time when they shine and you will see all of their amazing capabilities, just as people did with me when I was a baby.

Chapter Six: Black Scribbles

Crying is learning and crying is growth. All we need is patience.

When I first began elementary school, I was very happy. I really enjoyed the school environment and being around kids my own age. I have always loved learning, which meant that I was in my element at school. I was an outgoing little girl and I talked out in class all the time. This is very different from how I am now. I am actually the exact opposite. Elementary school is the only time I ever was an outgoing person, to a degree. I sometimes got in trouble for talking too much when the teacher was talking. I would get in arguments with my classmates because I did not hold back on saying exactly what I thought. I have always been a very literal and practical thinker and, even when I was in elementary school, I knew when someone was out of line and I didn't mind pointing it out. I was very clumsy. I couldn't do a lot of the things that the other kids could do either because of my clumsiness or because I was too embarrassed to try. I also didn't always think the way people might have expected me to. I wasn't diagnosed until I was in second grade, so in kindergarten and first grade, I was still seeing many doctors, being evaluated, and going through the process of figuring out what I needed in terms of services at school. For the most part, I was still a big mystery. I had a huge question mark lingering over my head and everyone was just trying to do their best at making sure I got what I needed out of school.

Even before I was diagnosed, I received services. I did occupational therapy once a week during my first and second grade school years. I remember doing many fun activities, such as weaving a skateboard through cones while on my stomach, stacking cups into a pyramid form, and playing a game called Rush Hour. It is one of my favorite games that comes with a bunch of cars, a track, and a stack of cards. When you pull out a card, you will see a picture of the cars arranged on the track and you have to take that same color car and place them on the track where they are in the picture. In every arrangement, there is a little red car that starts in the same exact spot every time. Your job is to get that red car out of the track by moving around the other cars that are blocking it without turning them. They have to stay in their lane either going up and down or side to side. It is like a puzzle that you have to figure out. I loved that game so much that my mom bought it for me and it still sits in my game cupboard. I get it out every once in awhile if my brothers start getting competitive because it is the one thing I can beat them in. It stretches your mind and it takes a lot of thought, which is just what I'm good at. I really like all sorts of puzzles, riddles, or engineer type things. For Christmas when I was in fifth grade, I got a Marble Works set. I learned how to build these awesome marble towers using all of the pieces, and then watching all of the marbles go down at once. I did that until I was older than I would like to admit. One day, I was well into high school and I set one up for the first time in a long time. My dad and Austin walked in the front door and said almost simultaneously, "That's so cute that you still play with that!" and "You're never too old to play with Marble Works!" Now I just build them for the kids I work with, but I definitely enjoy it when I do. There is something about building a Marble Works tower and being able to master the game of Rush Hour that comes naturally to me while it actually seems very difficult for a lot of other people. Once I get the hang of it, I pretty much become obsessed and it just starts to be second nature for me.

In high school, one of the aides in my resource class, Mrs. Byker, had a binder with mind-puzzles in it for when students were done with their homework. There were approximately forty total puzzles in her binder and I did them all multiple times. It was one of my favorite things about high school, if I'm being honest. It would start with a story you had to read and then it would give you some clues. For example, the story might have talked about four different people who were at the county fair, and it would say they all ate four different foods, drank four different drinks, rode on four different rides, and entered four different contests. Then, it would list the four different foods, drinks, rides, and contests and, by reading the clues, you would have to figure out which person ate which food and so on. There were a few that I got stuck on and Mrs. Byker had to get out her answer sheet, but I loved to do them because it stretched my mind. I had pretty much gained a certain amount of fame among the other kids in my resource class for being able to figure out these puzzles. Sometimes, I would hear Mrs. Byker say from across the room, "Jilly! We need you!" and I would walk over to help her and one of my classmates figure out a puzzle. Rush Hour, Marble Works, and the riddles/puzzles Mrs. Byker kept in her binder were great ways for me to exercise my brain.

When I was in kindergarten, there was an aide in my classroom who actually worked one-on-one with another student, but she also helped me a lot too. I had certain sensory issues, but I also had certain sensory things I loved. I loved to have my arms tickled and, when I was really little, I used to sit on my grandma's lap while she rubbed my arms for me. It calmed me down incredibly and I almost went into a trance when she did it. Even into high school, when I was really upset, I would ask my mom to rub my arms. I figured it would be a good way to help me calm down, but she was always in too much of a hurry to sit down and rub my arms. I don't know what it was about the feeling, but it had an effect on me. I was normally a child who was constantly moving from one thing to the next, never giving my brain a break, and only wanting to move at the fastest pace possible. This was one of the only moments where I would completely calm down when I was this age. They implemented the rubbing of my arms into my kindergarten classroom and the aide for the other student, Mrs. Hackett, would sit with me one-on-one while she ran a special brush up and down my arms and legs. It had the same calming effect on me, and it really helped me to have a moment where I could decompress and separate from the hustle and bustle of the kindergarten classroom I was in.

I remember having a hard time staying on task when I first started going to school, and my mind was always wanting to go into my rope world. That is still a fact in my life today. The more stressed out I am, the more my mind needs that time to do my rope and music and escape from the world for awhile. It is a very hard thing to balance, and I can imagine it will only get more difficult as I get older. The feeling of needing to do my rope and my music affect absolutely everything I do. Pretty much any moment where my brain is not being stimulated at the rate I would prefer it to be, my mind is trying to go into my rope and music world. For example, if I am in class and I don't feel like I am learning very much at any particular moment or I am not very interested in what is being discussed, my mind will be pulling me towards that world and that tense feeling will build up inside me until I can release it. Another example would be grocery shopping with my mom. (She is the slowest shopper ever!) Those kinds of things will always be a struggle for me. There is at least one moment every single day where my mind is pulling me towards that world, but I am unable to do my rope or music at that time. Because of this, when I was in kindergarten, being brushed on my arms or legs gave me a minute where I could relax. Doing this didn't take the place of doing my rope or music. It does not have the same effect by any means, but it did make it easier for me to get through the day when I was unable to do my rope or my music. It distracted me from those feelings for at least a few minutes during the school day.

I have offered this as a piece of advice before to a mother of an autistic child. She said that every few minutes, her son needed to run. He could hardly get through the school day or a meal or a movie because of it. It pretty much clicked with me instantly that what her son was feeling was probably very similar to what I feel. When I was that young, I would not have been able to regulate this feeling as well either. It made perfect sense to me. I have an extremely hard time sitting through an entire movie. If I am in the movie theater and I know it isn't exactly possible to do my rope or music at that moment, it is different. It is a lot like a bad habit because the only way to be feasibly kept from stimming is to know that I can't. However, if I try to watch a movie at home with my family, I will almost always excuse myself about forty minutes into it because I just can't sit there like that. Even if my mind is distracted by a movie, the thought is lingering in the back of my head that my room is right down the hall and my rope is in there. I told this mother I experience what I thought to be a very similar thing as her son. I explained to her that finding something like my special brush that could be used while he was at school could be very helpful. It allowed me to relax, it released my tension for the time being, and it helped me get back on course. Part of my autism is being in a battle with my own mind. I just have to find the tools to combat it for a little while.

When I was in kindergarten, I was learning a lot, but I was also in an environment that was a lot more overstimulating than I was really used to. I had a lot of new people around me and, when I was in preschool, my mom was my teacher so I was used to being with her while I was at school. I have always been someone who likes a tiny bit of challenge in my life, though, and I definitely love to learn. I like to think of challenges as opportunities for learning. I remember a moment in kindergarten where my teacher, Mrs. Boles, put all of our names up on the board so we could learn to write them. I already knew how to write my name and I did it all the time. Because of using that elephant alphabet puzzle with Grandma Howard, I also knew all of my letters and I could read the names of the other kids, so I knew which name belonged to whom. I remember writing down every other name on my paper except for mine. I have also talked about the fact that I love names and words and this was right there on my list of favorite things to do. To others, it might have looked like I was being defiant, but it was actually the fact that I was trying to challenge myself. Writing down my own name was no longer a challenge for me at all and, since I had this odd fascination with names, I took it upon myself to learn how to write everyone else's name as well. Those days I had with my Grandma Howard before I started school were vital for me in this way.

I was actually a year behind in school. I could have gone to kindergarten a year earlier than I did. My birthday is September 6th and, at the time, that date met the cutoff. But all I could do was scribble with a black crayon. I shouldn't say that is all I could do, rather, it was all that I *would* do. It is funny to me when I hear that story because I know I had SO MANY things going on in my head. I had a lot of things that I knew how to do. I mean, I could say the alphabet backwards, for example. But all I would do was scribble with a black crayon. My grandma had sat me down at the table the year before I was originally scheduled to go to kindergarten and she had tried to see what I could do. That was all I would give her and she told my mom I wasn't ready for kindergarten. She had me wait another year and start when I was only a couple weeks away from turning six. It ended up being a good thing because I had another year to prepare for school, but scribbling with a black crayon was definitely not all that I could do. I was able to do a whole lot more than that. I was just still stuck inside my own head. I hadn't shown them all the things I could do yet. I was learning and processing and reciting and picturing and humming and memorizing. I think it is just another example of what I have always liked to say: autism is more than meets the eye. What you see is only a small sliver of what you *can* get. And what you do get is hardly ever the whole thing. There is always more. There are layers upon layers of things going on inside our heads. There are stories and scenarios and pictures and categories and words and songs and numbers and letters and movies and places that only we are capable of going. There are thoughts that have the potential of amazing the entire world, but a lot of us aren't capable of easily letting them show, or even giving them any air at all. We may seem like we have nothing to say, or maybe nothing *important* to say. But once you get to know us, you see an almost completely different person with a lot to offer and a ton of things to show you and tell you.

For calendar every day, Mrs. Boles had little laminated paper frogs on a large ring and each frog had somebody's name on it. She would flip it over everyday to find out who would be her calendar helper that day. I always looked forward to reading the name in the morning and, even into first and second grade, I would purposely peek in her windows to see what name was on the frog. For Christmas, my parents got me my own laminated frogs and a ring at a teacher store and I wrote all of my classmates' names on them and took them for sharing. Mrs. Boles also had little clothespins with our names on them up on the calendar board and I got those for Christmas as well. And, yes, I wrote everyone's name on them. If you look in our kitchen cabinets, you will still see names of my classmates on the clothespins holding the powdered sugar and the chips in place written in my little five-year-old handwriting. When I started memorizing my brothers' yearbooks, I cut up little pieces of paper and wrote all of their classmates' names on them, threw them in a basket in my room, and used to pretend that they were my "students" when I played imaginary school. I don't know why that has always been something that interested me so much, but I have always loved the concept of writing words, and names in particular, along with saying them. It was really nice when I think back on it to see how my parents and teachers humored me in this way. The afternoon kindergarten teacher, Mrs. Gross, who shared a room with Mrs. Boles, printed out a paper with the names of all of her students on it and gave it to me as a gift. I remember being so happy and taking it home just to copy all of the names down on another piece of paper. I have learned about this in my Child Development classes recently. When a child says, "I am going to be a dinosaur when I grow up," you should say, "Wow! What kind of dinosaur are you going to be?" Some people might want to say that becoming a dinosaur is impossible, but the best teachers are the ones who keep that spark alive for their children. When they bought me laminated frogs and clothespins for Christmas, and when Mrs. Gross printed out a paper with all of her students' names on it, they were all keeping that spark alive. It might have been a little bit more unusual than wanting to be a dinosaur when I grow up (maybe?), but it was what humored me. It was what I liked and what I thought was fun. Taking that seriously for any child is probably one of the best things you can do.

In my first grade class the following year, all of us kids had our own "schedules" to follow during center time. There were certain times where certain kids were supposed to be at seatwork and others were supposed to be reading and others were supposed to be at the teacher's table. Everyone knew their schedule and it was mesmerizing to me how that worked. My mom's cousin, Laura, was my teacher and she printed out the paper she had of everyone's schedule and gave it to me one day. I remember bringing that home, getting on the computer, and typing it up word for word. Nobody knew I was autistic at that time. Nobody knew why I liked names and words or why I thought that rewriting them was great fun. They all knew I was a little bit different and I needed a little bit more help and assistance, but I was still in the process of a diagnosis. It would be another year before I officially received it. Yet, they all did these things for me and now I know how important it was that they did so.

Laura taught all of my siblings and a lot of my cousins when they were in first grade as well. She was an amazing teacher and my grandma, my mom, and my aunt Laurene all used to volunteer in her classroom when I was in there. It was always fun for me to see them during the day, but my mom got to witness things I did that were different. She obviously already knew that because we were right in the middle of figuring out what my correct diagnosis was. But, by being in the classroom with me, she got to see how I was in that type of a setting compared to the other children. In the home, kids act differently than they do in a school environment, and if you only ever see them at home, then you might not necessarily notice the differences the way a teacher will. Seeing them in a place where they aren't as comfortable while also seeing them around the other kids will sometimes make those differences more noticeable.

I remember very vividly a day in first grade where I really had the urge to do my rope. I must have been overstimulated or anxious about something and, at that age, I hadn't yet completely cultivated the ability to do it in my head subtly. I was at Laura's center and I had to read a page aloud out of the book we were reading. Somehow, I tried to make my humming noise and recite the words on the page at the same time, which probably sounded really weird. Nobody knew it at the time, but what I was doing was putting the words in the book onto the pictures I had in my head. At the time, I probably only really had the pictures on my grandparents' refrigerator in my mind, but I had them memorized in order. I knew that Lindsey's tennis picture came right before Ethan and Austin's football pictures and then there was a picture of me at preschool and then one of Natalie and Blake at swimming lessons. There was one of my cousin Remy in the pool with my uncle Ron, and there was one of my cousin Rebecca as a baby. Those pictures are all still on the fridge, though they have been rearranged, but when I was in first grade, they were all I had to picture in my head. This was probably the first time I ever tried to consciously do my rope in my head, but I was unsuccessful. It sounded really weird and I got a few odd looks and a few laughs. I hadn't even thought that it would sound weird because it was so normal to me. I also probably based it's normalcy on the way my family reacted to it, which wasn't much of anything. They all just accepted it. I just figured everyone else would too, but the response I got from the people around me was one of the first inclinations I had that maybe what I thought was so normal was odd to other people.

Once I got a little bit further into elementary school, I sometimes had trouble wanting to go. I remember the first time I didn't want to get out of the car and walk into school really well, and it was the beginning of years of anxiety surrounding school that I would experience. My grandpa used to drive us all to school in his baby blue Crown Victoria that, years later, was given the name Vicky by Blake when it became his car. Lindsey was in college and moved out by the time I was in second grade, so Ethan, Austin, and I used to walk down to my grandparents house every morning before school. Then, we would drive the short distance to the other end of the property where Blake and Natalie would hop in the car. My grandpa would drive us to all of our destinations, which consisted of the high school parking lot for Ethan and Natalie, the middle school drop off zone for Austin and Blake, and the elementary school for me. I remember once after Ethan and Natalie got dropped off, we were parked outside of my school, Mill Street Elementary. I was watching the kids in my class play outside and I was crying because I didn't want to go in. Eventually, my grandpa drove away with me still in the car, we finished the drop offs, and he took me back home. When this happened, it was most likely the result of a tiff I had gotten in with one of the girls in my class. I have always been a very sensitive person; I get my feelings hurt really easily, and I think way too much about every little comment people make until it drives me crazy. I am a lot better about it now, but back when I was in elementary school, somebody could say something like, "Jillian thinks she is all that," and I would be afraid to go to school for weeks. That really happened. (Literally, I wrote my mom a letter that said I was never going back to school because someone said I thought I was all that). I have never seen anybody else quite like me in this way. I think it was a very extreme sensitivity mixed with a lot of predisposed anxieties I was already dealing with. But I didn't know how to handle them let alone understand what they really were or why they existed in me. I had a lot of anxiety about fitting in and being liked by the other kids, so maybe when something happened, I thought of it as a failure in that regard. I don't know exactly why it happened, but any little thing that was said, any little look that was aimed at me, and any little second-grade-girl dig was comparable to the end of the world as we know it for me. It deeply affected me every single time and I would really take it to heart. When I was in elementary school, and even middle school, I didn't have the ability to hold it in. I would just turn into a crying mess. Especially in middle school, I sometimes was unable to stop myself once I had started, and it would throw me into a bout of exhaustion and I would end up sleeping it off for the next couple of days. It was no joke. I have never, ever seen anyone else as sensitive as I was. It was always the start of a hurdle I would need to jump. It was the beginning of a bad couple of weeks. It always ended up with a conversation with my teacher and my parents and days of having to force me into the classroom.

Chapter Seven: Dealing The Emotion Cards

It is okay to take a break. We need time to reset.

When I got to third grade, I transitioned to another school, Fairview Elementary. I grew up in a small town and most of the kids I graduated with had been going to school with me since kindergarten. The elementary schools are broken up into two schools, Mill Street and Fairview, and in third grade everyone transitions together. My mom had been told by doctors to send me to a school where I never had to switch, but she decided against that and it ended up being a good thing. I am able to handle change a lot better than I think I would be able to had I never transitioned schools. Even though I may not always like it, I can do it because I have been experiencing it since I was little. Usually, when I transition from one school to the next, it comes with a lot of anxiety, as it does in most people, but it takes a little bit more getting used to for me than it might for others. I live on being comfortable, I absolutely hate being pushed out of my comfort zone, and I do my best when I know I won't be. Being in a situation where I don't know what is going to happen next can feel very unsafe to me. If I feel like something may happen that is going to make me uncomfortable, I will look for ways to get out of the situation. I have experienced lots of social mishaps in my life or things that make me cringe to think back on. When I am comfortable, however,

I can handle those things one thousand times better. I will mess up significantly more when I am on edge and nervous, and when I have those feelings people don't usually see the real me. People that have met me over the years and have gotten to know me quite well could probably tell you I was hard to talk to at first. I am extremely guarded and I am always trying not to say the wrong thing when I first meet someone. I am probably very awkward to talk to because I am so nervous. But once I get a little bit more comfortable, it is almost like I am a whole new person. I am able to have conversations much more easily and I am a lot more laidback.

However, there are people in my life who I have been around for as long as I can remember and I still don't feel completely comfortable when I talk to them. I think it is the context of where I am having a conversation. For example, at a family party, I am always nervous. There are A LOT of people in my family and when we have parties we are usually always packed tightly into a house. We have family parties every few months. We have one for Easter, Fourth of July, Thanksgiving, Christmas, graduations, and anything else that comes up that is worthy of celebrating. The host of the party usually changes with every holiday. Fourth of July is always at my grandparents' house while the others are typically hosted by my Aunt Laurene, Aunt Debbie, Aunt Julie, or Laura. The setting of the party usually has a big impact on my comfort level. When it is at my grandparent's house, I am only nervous about the social part. I am the most comfortable I could possibly be in that situation. When it is at someone else's house, it makes it a little bit more nerve-racking for me. I'm not only nervous about the people; I am then also uncomfortable with the setting. You wouldn't think that I would be. I mean, I have been going to all of these houses my entire life and I have been around all of these people since I was born. They all know me, love me, and accept me. But it is normally a very straining few hours for me, and if you asked the members of my family, they would probably tell you that I hardly did any talking or I only talked if I was spoken to. I observe conversations a lot more than I engage in them, especially in a party setting such as this.

A couple of years ago, Lindsey decided to do a three-generation podcast with her and I, our mom, and our grandma. It was a book club made into a podcast. We read a book over the course of a month and then we recorded ourselves having a conversation about it. It will be a pretty cool thing to be able to listen to years from now. We only did it for three months and then life got busy, but it was fun while it lasted. In January 2019, we posted the first one online and a lot of our family members listened to it. My grandma reported to me that four people in our family who listened to it didn't recognize my voice, and it took them a few minutes to realize it was me. That made me sad. It isn't that they did anything to upset me, but it made me realize even when I think I am making a lot of strides in terms of social interactions, I still have a lot of work to do.

When I went through my first huge transition of changing schools, I kind of fell back into myself. In kindergarten, first, and second grade, I had friends in my classes who I would play with at recess and I would talk to in class. I don't know if I actually felt completely accepted by some of them, even at that age, but I at least had someone. In third grade, I didn't really have anything to do with anybody. I still associated with my classmates while we were in class and I talked to them when they talked to me. But for the most part, I was happiest when I was alone. At recess, I only ever wanted to swing on the swings. That was all. I didn't want to play games with the other kids, and I certainly did not want to climb on the monkey bars. I have always had an innate sense of what is safe and what is dangerous, which has probably saved me from a lot of things over the years. I knew I was not coordinated enough for the monkey bars. I couldn't get a firm grip on them and I wasn't strong enough to hold onto them. I couldn't physically take one hand off of the monkey bars in order to grab the next one and move down the line. I could basically hold onto one monkey bar and just hang there for a few seconds until I let go or lost my grip. Also, there were three entire grades of kids (third, fourth, and fifth) all out at recess at once, and so there were a lot of kids climbing all over and running around. It was too much for me. I didn't want to get onto the play structure when there were so many other kids on there at the same time. I couldn't control if they bumped into me or if they ran by me super fast, which seemed like torture to me at the time. Therefore, to avoid that mess completely, I just stayed on the swing set. As soon as another kid started to count on me to get a turn with the swing, I would get off before they even finished and walk over to the person who had been on the longest (I usually paid attention). I would count on that person, and get right back on another swing. The swings were almost another way I could do my music. It was the physical movement involved in the swings that I just loved, so it helped me escape a little bit, even without the music. I was kind of able to let my mind go into my imaginary world while I was there on the swingset. Later in my life, roller coasters would become another perfect way for me to be able to escape without the music and just with the physical movement.

I think the reason I only wanted to play by myself was because I was really starting to notice my own differences. I didn't always think that what the other kids liked doing was fun; I liked doing what I liked doing and they didn't think *that* was fun. I started to feel like every time I tried to interact with my peers, it was a lot more difficult than when I just played by myself. I just wasn't the same as the other kids in a lot of ways and I would end up frustrated a lot of the time because I was just so confused on how to interact with them. The slightest thing had the potential of making me very upset and I would not be able to come back to school for weeks (not without giving my parents a lot of trouble anyway). I was diagnosed by this time; however, I was completely mainstreamed. I didn't spend any time in the special education classroom unless I was having a really, really hard time. I was nearly crippled with this fear of messing up around my peers, doing the wrong thing, or being put on the spot, and the best way to avoid all of those things was to not engage at all.

I knew I had autism and I was starting to learn a little bit about my struggles and my differences. I was almost proud of it and I hadn't yet noticed the stigma surrounding these kinds of disabilities. However, all it took was once. I had a girl I was friends with in fourth grade and I confided in her about my autism one afternoon while we were waiting for our parents to pick us up. She got mad and told me that she didn't like "those kinds of people." I was incredibly insulted, probably had a panic attack upon arrival at school for the next several mornings, and, after that, my autism was a secret. I didn't tell anyone, I never talked about it with anybody, and I hated that word. For the next several years, if I was having a conversation with a teacher or one of my family members, I would never say the word "autism." I would say "what I have" or "my disability." And it wasn't that girl's fault completely. I was friends with her throughout middle school and she was only a little kid when she said that. It was just the first realization I came to that I was different and that wasn't always deemed a good thing.

In third grade, I had a lot of trouble going to school. It was my first horrible year in terms of the anxiety I experienced surrounding school. I would wake up in the morning and cry because I knew what was coming. I hated school and I never wanted to go. I wanted to be at home with the people who knew me and accepted me. I wanted to be doing my rope and my music. In the mornings, I would do my rope and my music for about thirty minutes to be able to let it all out before the school day. That's still what I do if I have somewhere to go. When my dad would come in my room to turn off my music and have me start getting ready, they usually had the first inclination of what kind of a morning it was going to be. I didn't want to stop doing my music. I didn't want to go to school. At the time, I didn't know why I was afraid, and I couldn't express to anyone what was bothering me. As a result, I would just cry. The thought of school sent fear all through my body and being anxious only made me feel the need to do my music even more. I was afraid of the people I was around at school, students and teachers alike, but not because they were scary by any means. The kids I went to school with were not bad kids at all and my teachers were wonderful. Bullying was not an issue for me. I would not have wanted to go to school anywhere else. However, it was those few times that someone did say something mean or hurt my feelings that would ruin a huge portion of school for me. Though it was never that big of a deal, it seemed like the end of the world to me. My classmates didn't know any better. They just saw me as their classmate Jillian who was a little bit quirky and cried a lot. For the most part, they didn't know I had any kind of a disability at all. It was just my own underlying knowledge that I was starting to become more and more noticeably different. I was starting to feel it so much more than I ever had before, and it was starting to become a lot more difficult for me to handle it when things went wrong.

I have learned over the years that my disability seems to become more prominent in people as they grow older, and the way that others think about us tends to change a little bit. At least in my case, I felt like I kind of turned and went in the opposite direction of where I had been going. I had finally gotten the diagnosis my mom had been looking for, and I was recognized as a child who needed some accommodations and services. I started to come out of my shell and I was comfortable letting people know that I had autism. I was also comfortable talking about my rope and actually letting people see me stim out in public. Then, I started to get older and it got a little bit weirder to be doing the things I was doing. My rope was always a little bit odd, but the behaviors tend to become more noticeably different the older you get. As that started to happen, I kind of went back into my shell. I made my rope extremely private, I never wanted to tell anybody I had autism, and I stopped talking to people. I became super shy and afraid to have conversations with anyone. Sometimes, the negative responses I would get from people were well-meaning and normal, such as a teacher telling me to stop being disruptive, but they could change the tone of my day drastically and they actually somewhat changed my life drastically. Doing things that most people would deem socially inappropriate is kind of second nature to some people like me, especially when we are younger. When you do things that are socially inappropriate, you get negative responses. I think these negative responses are what caused me to change. That is a good thing in a lot of ways because it is how I was able to learn. I don't want to be known as socially inappropriate, but it also made me a lot more guarded and reluctant in terms of dealing with other people.

The world is not made up of people like me. I am a diamond in the rough, as far as I'm concerned. I have met, seen, and read about many autistic people. I went to school with some autistic people and got to know them personally. I have been able to work with some autistic people in the recent years. I see lots of similarities between me and all of them. I feel deeply connected to them on a different level than I feel with anyone else. But I am autistic the way *I* am autistic. Those people are autistic the way *they* are autistic. I am a twenty-one year old working college student with autism. I was a little third grade girl with autism at one time. Completely mainstreamed, nobody could tell I was autistic, and nobody knew how deeply they were affecting me. They didn't see the battles I was fighting in my own mind. I was held to a certain standard. I was expected to know how to sit still. I was expected to know what to say and what not to say, but there were times where I just couldn't meet those expectations. Those things don't always come naturally to me the way they do to most people. I didn't even know what it meant to be socially inappropriate. I didn't know that there were standards and I surely didn't know I was not meeting them. I was outgoing, I was completely out of my shell, and I was comfortable with how I was. Then, suddenly, I wasn't like that anymore. I turned into a different person. I worried constantly about saying or doing the wrong thing. I didn't want to get a negative response. I was a hermit in my shell only letting a few people in and not letting anyone see the disability side of me. I kept it hidden as best as I could. My autism was a secret for not a soul to know about. I was embarrassed of it. I would never even think of raising my hand in class out of fear of getting a negative response from someone. I didn't want to meet new people. I wanted to stay in my comfort zone. I had a lot of anxiety about going places and doing things. I just wanted to fall back into the shadows and not be seen, heard, or looked at. I completely shut down, and it has taken me years to try to reverse that. It is still something I am always working on.

On a typical day in elementary school, my dad basically had to force me to get out of the car and go inside. I gave both of my parents a really hard time when they would drop me off because I was just so terrified of school. By this time, my grandpa didn't take me to school anymore because all of my siblings and cousins were able to drive themselves. It was probably a really good thing because I ended up taking a very long time to get dropped off at school every day. I would cry the whole ride into town and then I would have a complete meltdown when the school came into view. When Christmas break was approaching, my third grade teacher, Mrs. Sorenson, had us write down our New Year's resolutions. I remember writing down that my New Year's resolution was to "come to school good for my dad." I am pretty sure that didn't work out for me, but at least I had the mindset that it could get better. It also showed that I didn't want to be doing that. I didn't want to have such a hard time going to school and I didn't like it at all that I made it harder on my parents. If I could have helped it, I would have never had that kind of trouble going to school. It was a fear that was so intense I couldn't control myself, and it wasn't a matter of simply getting over it. It was a mountain to climb every single day, and there was no other way to make me go than to force me.

When I was in third grade, though I was mainstreamed, I still got some special services. I had these pads I used to sit on. When I was in second grade, they had tried to give me a workout ball to sit on instead of a typical desk chair. These pads had the same kind of purpose, but they were a lot less noticeable. They just sat right atop my chair. I had two and they were different shapes. One of them was just a circle and the other was elevated. One side of it was a bit higher than the other and it slanted down. They worked well for me and all of my classmates always wanted turns with them. I also had what I called "emotion cards." They were pictures of people with facial expressions showing many different emotions. Sad, happy, anxious, angry, tired, etc. The point of them was for me to hand to my teacher if I needed to express to her that I was feeling a certain way, but I didn't know how to explain it verbally. I only had to use them once when I had brought my Jonas Brothers magazine for sharing and I handed Mrs. Sorenson the "nervous" card. There were probably a lot of other times I could have benefitted from using them, but this particular time, my mom had known I was nervous upon drop-off and encouraged me to show Mrs. Sorenson my nervous card. It was something I might not have thought to do on my own. I remember one of my classmates seeing these cards in my desk one day. They were tied together by a rubber band and the sad face was right on the top of the pile. When he asked me what they were, I got embarrassed. I knew that those cards had something to do with my autism, and my autism was not something that I wanted anyone to know about. I remember replying to him that they were "a card game." He was a third grader so he was satisfied with that answer, but it scared me. I knew that none of the other kids had to have emotion cards in their desks in case they got to the point that they couldn't speak to explain what was wrong. It was only me and I didn't want them to find out I was different. I just wanted to blend in with all of them.

In fourth grade, there was a psychology intern who would meet with me every Wednesday. We used to play a lot of fun games, just like I had done with my occupational therapist in the years prior. I still have a box we made in my desk drawer. We put little slips of paper with encouraging words in it so that I could take one out and look at it when I was feeling anxious or upset. I also remember getting to interview all of my family members about their favorite thing to do, their full name, birthday, etc., and then I came back the next week and reported all of my findings. I thought that was the best thing ever, and after meeting with her for a few months, she gave my class a lecture on autism. She taught them about what it was and she told them that their classmate Jillian actually had it. I wasn't in the room at that time because they thought it would make me uncomfortable (which it definitely would have), but I remember thinking it was kind of special. I think they probably thought it was a good and necessary step for me. I still had all of my reservations about wanting to let people know about my autism. I wasn't ready to talk to people about it just yet, and I wouldn't be for a few years, but it was kind of a small step in the right direction. It was a little bit of acceptance for myself and that was something that I needed.

I got to go to the special education classroom a couple of times when I was in fourth grade. Once, I had gotten dropped off at school and I was late. I didn't want to walk into my classroom because I knew that everyone would turn around and look at me. I was standing outside the door crying and I didn't know what to do. I probably would have just stayed there until recess. Ever since about third grade, I have always had a horrible fear of being the center of attention or having all eyes on me. Like I said earlier, I don't want to be noticed in a room full of people. I am too afraid of getting those negative responses. I have a lot of fear of being laughed at, rejected, or made fun of in any way. None of those things happened to me very often. Maybe they did a few times here or there, but it was pretty rare. But, if I'm being honest with you, I think I know why they didn't happen very often. It is because I prevented it the best I possibly could. Had I been someone that still wanted to talk out and say things I maybe shouldn't say, even after I got those negative responses, I would have gotten them a lot more than I did.

I have grown up with a keen sense of safety and a strong sense of myself. For the most part, I have been able to keep it all under control, and when I can't, it is very hard for me. I don't participate in things if I am scared of what could happen. If I can envision myself getting hurt physically or mentally, I will NOT do it. The times that it has happened to me have been the times where I either didn't see it coming or there was nothing that I could do to prevent it. Even now when I go to my college classes, I sit in the back near the door just in case something comes up that makes me uncomfortable and I feel like I have to leave. However, I don't like to sit right next to the door because I don't want to be asked to turn the lights off because everyone looks at you when you do that. I am one step ahead of uncomfortable situations and I am always looking for ways to prevent them for myself as best as I can.

The special education teacher, Mrs. Marzolf, knew who I was, of course, but she didn't work with me on a regular basis. On that morning when I didn't want to walk in late, she was walking down the hall and noticed me standing outside the door in tears. She stuck her head in the door and told my teacher she was taking me with her. We went to her room and she took me out to pick flowers. She had jars with bugs and plants in them and I sat and watched them. I had a horrible fear of praying mantises because of this one time when I was swimming with my cousins in the ditch and had about ten of them stuck to me when I got out of the water. I still haven't gotten over that fear, but, nevertheless, watching them through the plastic jar was just fine. I don't really remember Mrs. Marzolf asking me what had happened, and if she did, I can't be sure that I gave her the true answer or that I even answered at all. I still had that embarrassment of the things that upset me and the things that set me apart from everyone else. However, I haven't ever forgotten that day with Mrs. Marzolf because it made me feel so much better to be able to seperate from the kids in my class and go somewhere quiet and accepting for a little while. I was able to get my head back on straight before I started the day over again. In the couple of years that followed, the people around me would come to realize, and I would come to realize about myself, that sometimes that separation and quiet time was all I really needed.

The next time I went to Mrs. Marzolf's room, I had been asked to go up to the board and solve a math problem. If you know me, you know I didn't know how to do it. I have always struggled with math and I am much better at reading, writing, and spelling. Math has always been my hardest subject, especially if it has anything to do with algebra. If there was one type of math that I was a little bit good at, it was geometry. When I got asked to go up there and do the problem, I did it completely wrong and people laughed at me. I think I was probably about two-hundred numbers off or something very similar. By going up there to do this problem, I was vulnerable and that is what has always scared me. I was susceptible to the negative responses, if they came, by being up there in front of my class doing something I knew I wasn't good at. When people laughed at me, the world might as well have just ended right then.

At this time, nobody yet knew going up in front of the class was such a fear for me. And, of course, everyone shares that fear at least a little bit, but mine is a little bit heightened. It has the anxieties of autism thrown into it. Since it is something that most everyone experiences, and I hadn't yet been able to voice how much of an issue it was for me, it wasn't something from which I was exempt. My teacher was just doing what she would do with any of her other students and treating me like the rest of the kids, which is what I would have wanted her to do. Unless it was something that was in writing and they were expected to follow, I wanted them to do just what they would for their other students. I didn't want my teachers to feel like they couldn't get on me if I was in the wrong. I didn't want them to be afraid of crossing me, even though *I* would have been afraid of crossing me. I was very, very sensitive, so I could see where my teachers probably wanted to avoid that as best they could, but if I needed to be corrected, I know now that I should have been corrected. I have come to realize that those are the times we learn, even though it may be painful for us. I never want the fact I have autism to be the reason people don't want to talk to me a certain way or don't want to tell me certain things.

When I went up in front of the class to solve that math problem, I remember exactly who it was that laughed the hardest. In high school, I experienced two classes where he sat right next to me and copied my every move onto his own paper while I pretended not to notice. Interesting how things turn out! Anyway, it hurt my feelings and it was one of those times where I could not hold it in. I got very upset and my mom had to come in the next day to talk to my teacher about it because, of course, I didn't want to go to school. When my teacher, Mrs. Foster, noticed that I was crying, she wrote a little note on a piece of paper and asked me to take it to a certain room, which happened to be Mrs. Marzolf's room. She knew I knew whose room it was, but none of the other kids did. Once I got there, Mrs. Marzolf did the same thing with me that she had done the time before, and it was a really great way for me to decompress both of those times.

Though I was completely mainstreamed in elementary school, there is no denying that having had those moments a little more often may have caused me less stress. I actually really think that it would have made things a lot easier for me. It may have made me less nervous to come to school if I knew I was going to get some time to relax in another environment that was not so busy. I remember when I was walking to the special education room with the note from Mrs. Foster in my hand. I was crying and I heard a car horn go off on the street near where I was walking. I turned and saw my grandma's brother, my uncle Larry Howard (I have three uncles named Larry so I have to be specific). He was at the stop sign across the street waving at me. My Grandma Howard was in the rest home just down the street from my school at the time, and I would assume that he was probably coming from there. I remember feeling happy and smiling as I waved back. It was a good reminder for me that I wasn't just a girl who was ultra sensitive, anxious, and scared, concealing my disability and trying to make it through the day. I was a member of this very large family and I was loved by them too.

Chapter Eight: Scissor Cutting

We learn in a different way. Sometimes, we need a little bit more coaching.

My teachers in elementary school were all amazing and did the absolute best by me that they could. Mrs. Boles, Mrs. French, Mr. Muser, Mrs. Sorenson, Mrs. Foster, Mrs. Neiss, and Mrs. Martinez all were amazing advocates for me and made my elementary school years, though they were incredibly difficult, a lot less painful than it would have been otherwise. For the most part, they worked very well with my mom and made sure that they listened to her every time she had to come to the school to advocate for me, which was very often. They also understood that I needed a little bit of extra love, even when I wasn't diagnosed yet. I can't stress enough how important that is. When you have a child like me, it makes a world of a difference when everyone can see past their challenges (such as crying at the drop of a hat and never stopping), and put their best foot forward anyway to ensure that they are successful. My life would have been incredibly harder had I not had the help that I did. Even though I didn't get the break that I think would have made things easier for me, I had teachers who cared to get to know me and learn to understand what I needed.

My fifth grade teacher, Mrs. Niess, really helped me with my transition to middle school. She wrote a very nice and informative letter to my future teachers explaining all of the things she had come to know about me. She seemed to have really understood what had worked for me in her classroom, and she had taken the extra steps to help me be more successful as her student. She wrote that paper to help me do the same in middle school. In elementary school, a lot of my issues were still up in the air, so to speak. I was only able to voice the bare minimum of what I was feeling and I was still a big mystery. A lot of the things I had a hard time with were completely unexplained. As a teacher, that would make it hard to ensure I got everything I needed while still succeeding in school. However, I was very fortunate to have teachers in elementary school who cared enough to try for me and I wish that everyone in a similar situation as me could experience the same.

I had to figure out who I was at a very young age and I had to try to understand my own mind, which hasn't been an easy thing to do. I have come to realize over the years that my autism tends to be a mystery for others around me. They don't understand why I can't do certain things because I look like I am capable of doing as much as anyone else. However, there are times where my autism is a mystery for me as well. Sometimes, I don't even know what is completely wrong with me and I have to ask myself questions before I can figure out what is going on, such as, "Are there are too many changes happening lately? Are my clothes too uncomfortable? Are the lights too bright? Did I get enough rope and music time this morning?" Typically, these can be factors as to why I'm more stressed out than usual. It is hard enough to have to worry about those things on my own and it makes it a lot harder when other people are not receptive to the fact that my struggles are valid, even if you can't see or understand them. If you are not autistic and you are looking at this from the point of view of a caregiver or a teacher, I would advise you to never make someone with autism feel like they are a burden for being autistic. Maybe you expect something more from them, but the fact is autistic people can't always meet your expectations. And you won't ever truly understand what it is like for us, but you can make our lives so much easier or so much harder depending on how you view our autism. I have come across people who have done both.

In fourth grade, I did a little bit better with my peers. I kind of came out of the "only wanting to swing" phase and I started interacting a little bit more with the other kids. I made a few friends with the people I sat near. My table always stayed the exact same with the same five kids sitting around it all year long. When everyone else's seats switched every few weeks, Mrs. Foster kept our seats the same. Now I understand why. She knew I was comfortable in that particular seat and next to those particular people and it made a lot of sense to just keep me there. I have always done better with consistency, and even though it could have been viewed as special treatment, I really benefited from that. Flexibility is something I have always had to work on. I would say that I do a lot better with it now, but when I was always nervous and on edge, change of any kind made things a lot harder for me. I am glad Mrs. Foster knew that and accommodated me because that seat is where I was comfortable, even though I didn't ever come out and say it. Sometimes, those little things that seem small and easy to most people can be hard for a person like me to do.

After my third grade year, the part of life I struggled with the most was my sensitivity and the need to do my rope and my music. I wasn't only wrapped up in my own head (on the swings), as I had once been, and I was a little bit more comfortable in my classroom. It probably had a couple factors: the particular group of kids I was with and the maturity I was gaining one slow step at a time. Sometimes, even the physical environment itself could make a difference for me. I can't say I was gaining a lot of understanding of myself, though I am sure that was slowly creeping in as well. However, I don't feel like I really began to understand a lot of things about myself until I was much older. I had situational anxieties, such as walking into the classroom late, but I hadn't yet fallen into the trap of intense, chronic anxiety I would experience in the next couple of years. All I knew at that time was I was different. I knew I had autism. I didn't completely know what autism meant, but I knew my rope and my music were a part of it. I knew I had a lot of emotional problems, such as my sensitivity. I knew the things that separated me from the other kids in my school. I wasn't like most of them and I already had come to terms with that fact.

There were lots of other changes going on in my life around this time as well. When I was ten years old, I got my first period. I knew what a period was, but I didn't know what it was going to be like. I saw it and I ignored it. I didn't tell my mom. I just kept changing my clothes until she noticed. Personal hygiene can be difficult for some autistic people. It doesn't exactly come naturally to some people with autism how you would take care of yourself in certain ways. Though it is embarrassing, I can attest that, for me, it did not. Without going into details, I will just say I needed a little bit more coaching in this area. When I was younger, I would go a week without showering if I could. I absolutely hated it. Once I got a little bit older, I began to really see the necessities around making sure you are clean or at least properly taking care of your hygiene. Now, I can't even go one day without showering or I feel completely thrown off. But back when it didn't matter to me, I was gross.

Some of the things most people just know how to do don't necessarily come easy to me. I have a harder time figuring out how to take care of myself than a lot of other girls might. I have always looked around at other people and heard their conversations, not just pertaining to hygiene, but also just lifestyle or household topics, and I am amazed at how it seems like they just get it. They just grow up and then it is almost like they just know what to do. They may need someone to show them how to do something or tell them how things go one time, but then it seems as though they can just do it by themselves. That has never been the case for me. I live off of a lot of trial and error experiences. I sometimes don't have the confidence to know that I can do something if I try hard enough. But, a lot of the time, my mind draws a blank in the areas where everyone else seems advanced. It is almost comical because a lot of people could not memorize all of the things I can memorize, but they are on top of their lives in areas I am just lagging behind. I can tell you exactly what I was doing on July 14, 2014 and June 5, 2017 and January 10, 2018, but it looks like a two year old made my bed. You want to know somebody's birthday? I can tell you. You want to rely on me to be able to mop the floor correctly? You're probably going to end up disappointed. A lot of this is due to the fact that I struggle with my fine motor skills A LOT, but some of it is also just the way I learn.

When I was first being taught how to put gas in my car, my dad showed me how to do it multiple times. He explained it as we were going through the motions, he demonstrated it to me, and I asked questions to make sure I was getting it right. However, I could never remember how to do it. I was just not learning it at all, and I would get frustrated because I would see the other kids my age fill up their cars with gas without even thinking about it. I finally said to my dad one night when we pulled up to the gas station, "Dad, can you just let me do it by myself and only stop me if I am going to blow something up?" He said that would be fine and he just stood back and watched me as I figured out how to do it. The next week, I was able to go get gas in my car by myself. I no longer needed the help. It is interesting to me how that worked because, while Lindsey, Ethan, and Austin all probably learned how to put gas in their car by my dad showing it to them the same way he had tried to do with me, I needed to try it on my own. I needed it to be shown to me a few more times than most, and then I needed to see what I could do. It just doesn't come to me the way it comes to most people. Sometimes, you might just need your grandma to ask you if you just got done washing your hair when, in fact, you did not. You might need to be reminded several times. It doesn't come naturally, and it may not come easy, but it can come if you put in enough practice. It is also important to have these kinds of things explained as thoroughly as possible for me.

There was one time in middle school that I stood at a door for about ten minutes trying to unlock it with a key. I didn't know how to do it. I have watched people unlock doors my whole life, and it is not that hard of a concept to grasp, but until I figure it out myself, I am not going to be able to do it at all. I have been given jobs to do before and I have ended up in a situation where I don't know how to tell someone that I don't know how to do those things because I know they are simple tasks to them. Taking out the trash is easy. Folding clothes should be fairly easy. It seems ridiculous to say that I wouldn't know how to do those things. But if I have never had the experience of doing it myself, my mind pretty much draws a blank to it completely. At the high school I went to, there is an ironing board in the Life Skills classroom that has the imprint of an iron burnt right onto the middle of it. It's my fault. I had never ironed before. I didn't know I had to stand it up when I was done. I told my friend it was me one time and she went, "OMG! We always make fun of the person who did that!" There are some things that just take longer for me to grasp while everyone else seems to already know how to do them and those things are frustrating for me.

Like I have said, my anxiety in elementary school was more situational. I didn't have a horrible amount of trouble unless something had happened. I basically took everything to heart. I could never turn my mind off. If I got in trouble, I would usually feel embarrassed at first, but I wouldn't necessarily get upset. But since I couldn't ever get myself to stop thinking about it, I would eventually lose it and it was very hard to get me to stop. I would do the same thing if I got into a tiff with another kid as well. Normally, when I think about the incidents that occurred in elementary school that upset me, I can kind of understand where the teacher or the other kids were coming from. I have gone on to work with children, and I sometimes find myself having to get on them for doing things very similar to what I did. Because of this, I can understand it from a teacher's perspective, and the kids I've worked with have kind of helped me understand it from my peers' perspectives too. It has made me extra sensitive to the kids. I have found myself not wanting to be too harsh, or even get on them at all in some situations, because I remember how traumatic it was for me. Whenever I come across a situation where I feel like I need to talk with a child or tell them to stop doing something, I try to understand it from their perspective. I try to think about what might have made them do whatever it was that they did and handle it from there.

It is inevitable that teachers don't always see everything that happens. A lot of times, the kids' thinking might be a lot more justified than we realize in the spur of the moment. I really try to remember that. I do this because when I think back on the times I had a meltdown at school because I got talked to (and this isn't only limited to elementary school), the worst part of it is to know I didn't always necessarily deserve it. I don't mean to sound entitled. Of course, I had moments where I did things that needed to be addressed, just like everyone else. But a lot of times I just wasn't understood. Many times, I got in trouble for things I didn't know how to handle at the time and so I tried to handle it in the wrong ways. And maybe it wasn't even that I was trying to handle a particular situation, rather, I might have just been simply trying to cope. There was a lot of tenseness in my life. A feeling in my body and my mind pulling me towards a world I couldn't be in right at that moment. My rope and my music were not available to me during the school day. I was also usually pretty stressed out at school, so the feeling of needing to do my rope and my music was very strong, which only added to my stress. I was constantly on edge because of this. This is probably one of the big reasons that any little thing could set me off. But, also, there were times where I just didn't know any better. My mind was not wired the way most of the other kids' minds were and my wiring was the misunderstood one. I didn't understand the things the other kids thought were simple, and they didn't understand how I thought. Just like hygiene, it doesn't come naturally. Life in general doesn't come naturally for me, as it sometimes seems to for others.

I got in trouble once because I was told to cut my paper. I was supposed to be cutting along the black lines and for the other kids, this insinuation was understood. To me, it meant just what was said: cut the paper. I cut it in half, through the black lines and across the picture. To a teacher, this can be seen as defiance and it was. I was kept in for recess that day and I get it. I can see where you might think you were just being flat-out ignored in your instructions, but I didn't completely understand what was being asked of me and I was doing what I thought I was supposed to do.

I also once almost got sent to the office because I threw a ball at somebody and it hit him in the stomach. Then, another teacher came over and took me by the hand. She told me I was going to the office. I ended up immediately having a meltdown and becoming inconsolable and so she took me to my teacher instead. Looking back now, it makes sense. The fact I was going to the office was already traumatic for me because I had never received such a severe punishment at school and I absolutely hated to be in trouble. She had also touched me by taking my hand and that made it harder for me as well. That probably added to the enormity of the meltdown. In this case, I had done something wrong. I shouldn't have thrown a ball at somebody and that is something that kids will get in trouble for. The problem I have with a situation like this, though, is that I am not a violent person. I am the opposite of it. I can hardly even touch a person abrasively let alone do it with the intention to hurt them. I just don't have it in me. When I threw the ball at him, it wasn't like I was trying to hurt him. He was someone in my class I knew pretty well and I was just trying to play with him. I mean, they all threw balls at each other when they played dodgeball. I didn't realize it was going to be such a bad thing for me to do and I was completely shocked when I got in trouble.

Most of the time, there are a lot of factors that go into it. Every aspect of the situation needs to be taken into consideration because I have come to realize in recent years that every aspect of the situation matters. I could have an extreme amount of anxiety one morning and resist going into school with everything I have. The next morning, I could waltz in there happy as can be. Maybe on my bad mornings, I hadn't slept well. More than likely, I had not gotten enough rope or music time and that always threw me for a real loop. Maybe I knew there was a change in my routine that day. Maybe there was an assembly or a substitute. It might have even been that I wasn't comfortable in my clothes, or I had gotten my feelings hurt the day before. Those kinds of things could easily interfere with my day and cause me to have a very different type of a morning than I would've if my routine had been knowingly the same. When my anxiety was situational, there could have been a number of things going on. Maybe it was very loud in the room that I was in. Maybe there were a lot of people crammed into a tight space. Maybe there were too many things going on at once in my general atmosphere that it became too much to handle. Those are times I could have acted out in ways I shouldn't have. That wasn't the case in the particular situation with the ball; I actually remember very clearly thinking about how much fun I was having right before it happened. Right when I did it, I saw the look on his face and I knew that I should not have done that. I don't remember there being any outside sources that could have influenced my choice. It was simply a mistake that I made and that is definitely going to happen too. But there are also going to be a lot of times where there are outside sources that do contribute to the choice.

When I was in kindergarten, I cut a girl that was sitting right next to me with the scissors I was holding in my hand. I did it because she was yelling. There have been multiple incidents in my life where I have accused people of yelling at me and they reply that they are, in fact, not yelling at all. I don't know why this is, but it definitely feels like yelling to me. In other words, this girl wasn't doing anything wrong, and she wasn't even speaking directly to me. However, it was probably all of the outside noise mixed with the fact there were a lot of chairs with children in them all huddled around this table, and I was trying to concentrate on what I was doing. Never in my life have I ever wanted to hurt somebody or intentionally done anything to do so. But these moments had the ability to bring out what seemed to be behaviors in me that weren't pleasant. I have apologized many times over the years for doing or saying things I shouldn't have when I was stressed. A lot of times, things that normally would not really bother me will become almost unbearable if I am already stressed. When I cut that girl with scissors, it was not something I would have ever even typically thought of doing, but it was every aspect of the situation that contributed to how I handled it. That is where that comes in. I had heard her voice many times before and I had never reacted like that. Had there not been so much noise and chatter and confusion, I probably would not have that story to tell because her voice would not have agitated me like it did. And obviously, as a kindergartener, I didn't know how to handle it.

It all goes back to things coming naturally to others whereas they don't for me and for many other autistic people. The concept of using your words rather than hitting, for example, may seem impossible to a child with autism because putting the words together to explain what is wrong when you are autistic can be very difficult. As a result, it isn't always as easy as just simply stating what you want from them. You may have to continuously work at it. It may seem very repetitive, but it is important to keep working with them. If they are anything like me, someone with autism will learn with their experience and their experience usually entails doing something over and over again. Eventually, you learn how to be autistic in a neurotypical world. Eventually, it will become easier to identify the feelings of overwhelming frustration, and with time, you will know how to handle those feelings before things get out of control. Just a couple of months ago, I was at the grocery store with my mom and we were standing next to the hot food section. For some reason, there was a very shrill noise coming from one of the machines back there and it was really starting to get to me. I could feel myself becoming increasingly agitated and that is when those meltdowns can happen. It seems a whole lot less likely for someone my age because, by then, meltdowns are most certainly not expected of you. After a few seconds, I just briskly yelled at my mom, "I have to move away from here!" and I walked a little ways down the store until I couldn't hear the noise anymore. When I was a little kid, who knows how that situation would have been handled. Now that I am older, I am able to identify the feelings that are coming into my body and taking control of my brain (because that is what they do!), and I am able to know how to remove myself from the situation. However, it didn't come naturally. It took a lot of work and a lot of meltdowns to get here. As we get older, we will start to understand ourselves the best we can, and we may learn how to better handle the things that this world provides that may be nothing to you, but are a heck of a lot for us.

Chapter Nine: Drop And Give Me Twenty

If you know it will happen, if you think it might happen, or if you want it to happen, just be prepared.

I transitioned into middle school in August of 2011. A few weeks before school started, I got to go into the school office and pick up my schedule. It was the first time I would ever be changing classrooms and teachers throughout the day. I was excited for it, but I was also intimidated. I have always been the kind of person who doesn't necessarily like change and I usually have a difficult time dealing with change when it happens, but I also have always thrived on a little bit of challenge. I think it is this inner sense I have that it is good for me and it is teaching me something. At the time, I may not have necessarily felt that way about transitioning to middle school, but I can tell you that doing so taught me more than anything probably ever has. Middle school was an adventure for me. Those are hard years for pretty much everybody, and I definitely was not exempt from the normal struggles that middle school brings. However, my first year of middle school was probably the first year in my life where I really came face-to-face with my differences. I started to notice the parts of me that stood out and were not the same as the other kids that I went to school with. I always knew I was different in terms of my sensitivity, my anxiety, and my rope/music, but it became more prominent when I transitioned to middle school. It didn't seem to me like it was as accepted anymore, as much as it may have once been, to be different the way that I was. It was getting harder.

When you have autism, there is a certain skill that comes along with it. Most autistic people have to do this in order to survive in our world. The term is called masking and it is essentially acting. The natural things that autistic people do are typically not accepted by the outside world. Stimming is one of those things. Saying whatever comes to your mind could possibly be another. As people with autism grow and mature, just like I did, they start to realize that these things that are so normal and necessary for them are not accepted by others. At least in my case, I know that this is why I started to mask and I think it is like this for a lot of other autistic people as well. Masking is hiding the parts of you that are autistic and not letting anyone see your autism. A lot of times, when an autistic person comes out and talks about their autism, people will say the words, "You don't even look like you have autism." Wouldn't you be shocked to learn that NOBODY looks like they have autism because autism doesn't have a look? There is a good chance that you have had conversations with autistic people and never even known it. A lot of people with autism are professionals at hiding their autism from you. That is what masking is. You have to stifle your autistic traits in order to be accepted in this world and it is a very hard thing to do. Though it seems to be necessary for a lot of us, I also think that it can be somewhat unhealthy at times.

Masking hit me full force when I entered middle school simply because the things that I did were getting to be less normal, so I was having to work harder at masking. However, there are times where masking will fall short and people will see your autism, even if they don't realize that is what they're looking at. It is a little bit different to stand outside your classroom crying in eighth grade than it is in third grade. It isn't as accepted to be escorted into class by your mom your sophomore year of high school as it might be in your elementary school years. I think that the differences I had got more prominent as I got older, but I hid them even better at the same time. The hardest part to come to terms with is that the problems do not go away. The struggles don't magically disappear with age. You just have to learn how to deal with them as you learn about yourself and why you do the things that you do. But the struggles are still there and they always will be. That is why it can be so hard when your peers are meeting certain milestones and you just aren't. You can be trying and trying and trying, but you just aren't getting there as fast as everyone else is.

I have had this feeling in many areas of my life growing up, but I think that middle school was the hardest time for me to deal with that feeling. I wanted to be accepted. I wanted to be liked. I wanted to be seen as equal. I didn't want to be seen as different. I wasn't yet at the stage in my life where I was able to look at myself and see the good in who I was. I was not yet aware of the positive things having autism attributed to me. I just saw it as a burden and an anchor in my life. I didn't want any of my peers to know about it. I was embarrassed by it and that was a problem because it was not going to go away and it was a significant part of who I was as a person. Every part of me and everything that I did had at least something to do with my autism. It was tied into all aspects of my life and it still is. It was present in my friendships and my relationships with my peers because it was literally who I was. If you took away my autism, I would be a completely different human being. Everything about me would change. It wasn't something I could just avoid, but I was trying my absolute hardest to do just that. I was basically running away from myself and who I was as a person, and it makes perfect sense to me now why I had so much trouble in middle school. I wasn't accepting myself, yet I was expecting other people to accept me. And I guess I figured it out the hard way that it needs to happen the other way around. *I* needed to learn how to accept who I was. I was the only one in control of when that happened, and I didn't get there for what seemed to be a very long time.

When I was in sixth grade, I started to experience a lot of teenage girl things I had never experienced before. I still had my ultra-sensitivity, and I didn't always understand why people said certain things or why they cared so much about things that didn't seem to matter as much to me. I didn't care about *who* I was friends with. It didn't seem that important to me what other people were doing, what they liked or disliked, or how they dressed. If they were nice to me, then I was going to be nice to them. I wasn't accustomed to this new sense of image that everyone else seemed to suddenly desire. Later in my life, I had moments, of course, where I wished I was as pretty as some of the other girls I saw, or that I was as well-liked as some of the people in my grade seemed to be. But in sixth grade, I was not worried about much other than making it through the day without having any problems and, later in the year, I was concerned about whether or not I would make it to school at all.

I only wore my hair in a ponytail. It was a part of my routine and it was what I felt the most comfortable in, but also, it was the easiest for my mom. I wasn't able to put my own hair in a ponytail until I was much older. I struggle a lot with my fine motor skills and I have always had trouble completing tasks that involve using my hands with smaller objects, such as a ponytail holder. It is just really complicated for me to maneuver my hands the way I need to, and it has always just been a lot easier for me to just accept assistance from someone else. One morning, when I was a senior, I was getting myself ready for school and my brother, Austin, had stayed the night at our house. My parents both left for work early, so we were the only ones home. I usually had my mom help me with whatever I was trying to do with my hair because, yes, I still needed that help. But, on this particular day, she was not there to help me. I was only straightening my hair, which I was perfectly capable of doing, but my bangs always gave me more trouble than I would have ever thought they would. It was something to do with the way I had to turn my hand while holding my hair with the other hand and also making sure that I didn't burn myself. Because, you know me, I'm an accident waiting to happen. It is a lot easier for me now but, at the time, I still needed help straightening my bangs. Austin was my only option for that help and I called him into the bathroom. His hands shook and he had a worried look on his face as he said, "I don't know how to do it. Is this how I do it?" I just said yes and accepted whatever he gave me. It wasn't my best hair day, but it would suffice and it made me feel good to know I had such a nice brother.

Another time, I was with my social learning therapist, Molly, and we were doing a "mock pullover." I was scheduled to get pulled over by the cops, so I could be prepared if it ever did actually happen to me for real. I had a car crystal gifted to me by my friend for my eighteenth birthday and it hung down off my rearview mirror. It is a beautiful crystal sparkling with all of my favorite colors. The day it was given to me, we were leaving for a trip to Montana for my cousin Annie's wedding, and I took it with me just because I loved it so much. Anyway, I loved the crystal, but I was worried it could possibly be considered an obstruction of vision, and I didn't want to risk getting talked to about it when I did my mock pullover. (I also had a huge crack in my windshield that was fixed a mere one day earlier!) When we got to where we were going, I fiddled with the crystal trying to get it to come off of my rearview mirror. I finally was able to remove it and I put it in my center console for safe-keeping. I then asked Molly if, when we were all done, she could put it back on for me. I should have known who I was talking to. My very own social learning therapist who sees my potential and is not about to let me get away with letting myself off the hook. She knows I can do it if I try hard enough, and she also knows I will give up easily if I think I can't do it. She very blandly said, "Why can't you do it yourself?" I basically just sighed and said, "Fine." After I got home that night, I fiddled with it some more and I was able to get it back on my mirror. It was almost like I had just become used to the fact I was unable to do many things, so letting someone else do it for me seemed like the justifiable thing to do. In more ways than this scenario, she, along with some of the other resource teachers I have had, have helped me realize that about myself as I have gotten older. Maybe it will take me an hour longer than it would take most people, but I will usually master it if I don't give up.

When I was in sixth grade, I was still unable to tie my shoes. I actually didn't learn how to tie them until I was in seventh grade. In elementary school, I only ever wore velcro shoes to avoid having to tie my shoes. By the time I got to middle school, velcro didn't seem like a reasonable option anymore, so my mom discovered a few pairs of shoes that looked like they were tied. They had the shoe strings strung through the holes and everything, but they were actually just slip-ons. The strings did not come undone. I actually could step on the strings and pull them and they would just bounce right back to their place on my shoe. It was a great solution, but it also was the beginning of the point I reached in my life where I had to conform to fit the views of others. It was kind of like that saying, "You can't fit a square peg in a round hole." This was just one of those times. And, while you definitely cannot fit a square peg into a round hole, the square peg just keeps on getting pushed. It tries to fit and it doesn't succeed. It moves, changes position, tries again, and doesn't succeed. It knows it doesn't fit into the round hole, but that is where it also knows it needs to go. It is where the world expects it to go. And it isn't the round hole that ends up needing to conform. It is the peg itself. Whatever little sliver of the peg can fit into the round hole, though, is where we can find a little bit of solace. It is the areas where we seem "normal." The underlying parts of the peg, the parts that are under the surface, the parts that nobody can see, are the ones that, despite the attempts, will not fit into the hole. Those are the parts that we have to conform, and we have to attempt to change about ourselves. We have to try to hide the fact we are indeed a square, and we just pretend that we are round. This is masking and it is all I ever did as a middle schooler.

In my case, I have a hard time with eye contact, but it isn't that significant of a problem for me. Unless it is someone I am very comfortable with, I usually let my eyes wander for a few seconds, and then I bring them back. I will sometimes fixate on one thing and go back and forth from that object to the person I am talking to. This is one of the many stereotypes surrounding autism. Most people portrayed as autistic in the media have noticeably poor eye contact because of this. However, some people with autism have very good eye contact while others may struggle with either too much or too little eye contact when having conversations. It is a very broad spectrum and these stereotypes cannot be attributed to all of us. That would be a part of the square peg that found its way into the round hole for me because I can cover up my struggles with eye contact well. My fine motor skill issues, on the other hand, are not as easy to hide. Tying your shoes was something most kids could do by that age and I was lagging behind and it was embarrassing for me. I didn't want people to know about it. I don't remember ever telling any of the other kids at school about my inability to tie my shoes. If they paid close enough attention, they may have noticed the fact that my shoes didn't actually require being tied, even though they looked like they did. However, I don't recall ever wanting to let people know this fact about me.

There was a girl who I had a few classes with in my sixth grade year, and she was a part of the group I hung out with at lunch time. She was somebody I would have considered to be a friend of mine at the time, but there were a few times where we didn't get along very well.

That is something I do not handle well. Any kind of an argument with anyone is a traumatic experience for me. I get very emotional about it and it is hard for me to get over it after it happens. In sixth grade, it was never that big of a deal, but any little thing that would be considered a bump in the road for most people was like a mountain to climb for me. It would cause me to have trouble for days. All of that made getting through those rough middle school years extra challenging for me, my parents, and all of the people working with me. One day, there was a group of people sitting on the bleachers in the gymnasium after we had eaten lunch, and this girl asked me to tie her shoe for her. I really do think that she knew I couldn't tie my own shoes just because we were what I considered to be friends. I don't remember ever letting her know that information, but I think that she knew it; however, I'm not sure if her intention was to humiliate me or not. I would like to think it wasn't, but that is what happened either way. It was a situation where I was stuck between a rock and a hard place. I knew I wasn't going to be able to tie her shoe for her simply because I didn't know how to tie shoes. However, I also knew that there was a group of people listening, and I didn't want to embarrass myself. I just went the honest route and told her in front of all those people I didn't know how to tie my shoes. I remember that she laughed and said, "You don't?!" and that was a really hard situation for me. I had let people see in where I didn't want them to and I had been laughed at. Hearing that I couldn't tie my shoes was, for them, seeing a glimpse into my different side, and now I knew that my different side was laughable to others.

    I didn't learn how to tie my shoes for another year after that when I was thirteen years old. I learned in my living room amidst piles of laundry waiting to be folded. My brothers were living together in an apartment about an hour away at the time and they were home for the weekend. Of course, they had brought all of their laundry with them. While they were working on folding their clothes, they were teaching me how to tie my shoes. I kept trying and trying and never getting it right. Austin went outside to get something out of his truck and when he came back, I had stopped trying, and I was just laying on the couch. He yelled, "Drop and give me twenty!" After that, I was determined to learn so that I didn't have to do any push-ups, and I did learn that day in the living room with my brothers. I have been tying my own shoes ever since. My grandpa has repeated the same words to me over the years every time I talk about something daunting happening in my life. He says, "You never thought you would ride a bike. One day, you just told yourself, 'I'm going to learn how to ride a bike' and then you did. You never thought you would be able to swim, and then you put your mind to it and you learned. You never thought you would tie your shoes and then you learned. That is just the kind of person you are." The last time he told me that was just a few weeks ago and we were talking about something a lot more daunting than any of those other tasks: getting through college. It shows me that, as autistic people, we will get older. What we think is important will change. There are always going to be people doing things we wish we could do. There will be things that seem easy for everyone else that are very difficult for us, but there will always be that push. It is just like my story about learning how to put gas in my car. I didn't like how it felt that everyone else knew how to do it and I just didn't. What that girl did to me in terms of tying shoes was not nice, but it encouraged me to learn and it gave me a little bit of a push to do so.

In terms of swimming, I was scared of it. I didn't want to swim in the deep end. I was deathly afraid of getting my face wet or putting my head under water. I didn't like the feel of my floaties on my arms. I would never put on a swimsuit so I just splashed around in my underwear until I was too old to do that anymore. My cousin Blake once put my floaties on his arms just to show me how easy it was. He swam all the way to the deep end and yelled, "See, Jillian? I'm doing it! It's really easy!" And I just remember shaking my head and saying, "No. I'm not doing that. It's not easy. No." I watched all of my other cousins close in age to me dive off the diving board and slide down the slide. I really wanted to be able do those things myself, but I was scared. One day, I was in the pool with just my grandparents a couple of months before I turned seven and I was swimming back and forth between them. Eventually, I realized that we had moved to the deep end. "I CAN DO IT!!" I yelled when I noticed I was swimming. Then, I turned into a fish (figuratively). It is actually funny to me how that has happened every time. I am scared of something, I want to learn how to do it, I finally do learn, and then I'm a whiz out of nowhere. I think it is the feeling of finally accomplishing something I was behind in. It hasn't ever mattered that it took me longer to learn how to do something. The only person that ever affects is me. What matters is nobody ever let me give up trying.

I have always had an extremely supportive family. I grew up on the same property with a lot of my immediate family members. I was with them all the time. They knew me and they knew I was behind in some areas, but they never once made me feel bad about it. They helped me learn. How did I learn how to ride a bike? My family helped me plant the seed in my mind while on our annual beach vacation. I came home and my grandpa and my cousin Remy walked next to me as I pedaled. How did I learn to tie my shoes? My brothers encouraged me and didn't let me give up when I wanted to. How did I learn to swim? My grandparents taught me and my cousin Blake encouraged me. There are lots of moments in my memory where a family member said, "Look. I can do it. It isn't that hard. This is all you have to do." That may sound like it isn't helping and maybe it doesn't *always* completely help, but it plants the seed. It is part of the push. I won't learn by being forced. I have to be ready to do it myself, but the seed is planted in my head for when that moment comes. It is so important to have a little bit of a healthy push, even if it doesn't necessarily feel good at the time or even if it seems pointless. Too much too soon will *not* help. It will make it worse. That is why it is important to understand it takes time. You have to work it in slowly and you have to take baby steps towards it. However, it will not happen on its own. Often times, we need an outside source to give us that push or help move us along, and it is so important that we are supported.

For the first few months of my middle school career, I did perfectly fine. I went to school every day without any problems, unless something came up situationally, and for the most part, I was enjoying myself at school. I have always done fairly well academically so that was never really the challenge. It was the anxiety and the social things that could really set me back. However, when February of my sixth grade year hit, things really went south for me. My anxiety became a lot more than just situational; it became a chronic form of anxiety that just didn't seem to be going away. At the time, I could have never even cohesively put it into a thought why I was having so much trouble. I most certainly could not *tell* you what was wrong, and I still don't completely know what it was that caused me so much trouble for the remainder of that school year and the ones to come. I think it had a lot to do with how hard it was for me to get through the day without my rope and my music and have to keep masking through it all. However, I can tell you that when I was in the middle of one of those moments where I was visibly very upset, I didn't even always know what it is that I was feeling. I have always tried to understand my own mind, and I have never really been able to come to a complete conclusion as to why I had some of the meltdowns that I had. They were very real meltdowns and the feelings that I had were valid, but it also may have seemed like it didn't make any sense because it was even hard to understand from my perspective.

I used to try to justify it with a reason that, when I think back on it, wasn't actually the complete truth. Not that I wasn't being truthful, but just that I wasn't understanding it the way it really was. At my brothers' football games when I was little, I used to tell my mom I was cold or hungry or that I wanted to sit by my grandma. She would say things like, "It is one hundred degrees outside, you just ate a hamburger, and you are sitting right next to Grandma." How was she supposed to figure out what the problem is when the explanation I was giving wasn't adding up? It is almost impossible. The real reason I was upset didn't have anything to do with whether or not I was cold, hungry, or sitting next to my grandma. I was just scared of the bleachers. I have always been afraid of bleachers. They freak me out, especially when I can see through the cracks by my feet to the ground below. It is a paralyzing fear for me. I will pretty much find my little spot on the bleachers and then not move unless I absolutely have to. When I was little, what I was feeling was actually fear of the bleachers, but I was trying to justify my anxiety with other explanations because *I* didn't even know why I was so nervous and that made it impossible to be able to communicate it to my mom.

When I was in sixth grade, I didn't understand why I was feeling the way I was. I just knew I was scared to go to school. Now, I can tell you I had an intense fear of all things social interaction, I was very afraid of messing up socially, and I was going to a place where nobody could help me with that. I could not avoid social interaction when I was at school and mishaps came with the territory. When mishaps did happen, it made getting to school a whole lot worse. Eventually, I started resenting the help that I *was* getting. It was part of my rejection of being different the way that I was. I didn't want any help. I wasn't someone who should be receiving that kind of help, but I wasn't going to get very far with those kinds of thoughts because the fact was I did need help. At my school, we had what were called "modified Wednesdays" where we got out for the day about an hour and a half earlier than normal so the teachers could have meetings. For a period of time, I didn't have any trouble on Wednesday mornings because I knew I wasn't going to be there as long as I normally was. But after a few weeks, I started having just as much trouble on Wednesdays as I did every other day of the week. I remember my mom saying she felt we had "taken a turn for the worst." That was one of the hardest things for me. I knew I was making my mom sad when she had to leave me at school crying every single day, and I felt like a complete burden. I usually was crying before we even left our house because I was scared, and she had to leave me in the hands of someone else when I was upset like that every single day.

The people she left me in the hands of my sixth grade year were Mrs. Bishop and Mr. Pfaff. I became a little bit less mainstreamed in middle school because I started having so much trouble. I still had all mainstreamed classes, but I spent a lot of mornings with Mr. Pfaff and Mrs. Bishop in the resource rooms. This was the first time I ever really felt a little bit understood. My family has always completely understood and accepted me for who I was, but when I had Mrs. Bishop and Mr. Pfaff as my teachers, I felt understood in a different way. My *autism* was understood and I hadn't ever really experienced that before. They both used to explain things to me in a way that helped me start to learn how to understand myself and what it was that I was dealing with. They thought I was funny when I was not trying to be funny, and they saw the good in me when a lot of other people I worked with saw me as a behavior problem or an annoyance. They have stayed in my life even after they were no longer my teachers, and they have continued to help me as I have grown up. Another thing they have always done, though, is tell it to me like it is. They seem to know when I can do better and they have always given me that push to do better. I think that they live by the mindset of, "Oh, you don't want to do that? Ok. Let's go try it right now!" But that is what I needed in a lot of ways, even if I didn't like it at the time.

There weren't very many days I made it into my first period English class the second half of my sixth grade year, and it didn't have anything to do with the class or the teacher. It was all of my underlying anxiety that seemed to be getting completely out of my control. It was a lot for me to make it onto campus, and the thought of having to go into class after getting onto campus was extremely anxiety provoking. Once I got to high school, I was able to kind of come up with a term for this type of anxiety I was experiencing towards school. I called it a "barrier." It was an appropriate term because it described exactly how it felt on my end. I wanted to walk into class, whether it was my sixth grade English class or any other class I had trouble with. I wanted in myself to be able to push through all of the anxiety and just walk through the door, but that was not my reality. I was in a battle with my own mind. Half of me wanted more than anything to overcome this, and the other half kept repeatedly reminding me of all the reasons why I should *not* overcome this. There were times where I would walk up to the door of a classroom with the intention to open it up and walk in, but then I would backtrack. It was like something was stopping me or standing in my way, but it was my own mind that was actually doing that to me. As I walked towards the door, I would be thinking in my head, "Just go in. It will be painful for a few seconds and then you will feel better. You will find your desk, you will sit down, the teacher will start talking, and everything will be fine." But then, as soon as I had that thought, my barrier would occur, and it would stop me from thinking that way. It would make thoughts creep into my head such as, "Everyone will look at you and see you have been crying. Something bad will happen. Remember that one time when you overcame this fear, walked in, and your chair was gone? When someone else was sitting in your seat? That might happen to you again. Everyone will stare at you. You might even run back out the door like you did last time and that will be really embarrassing." Then, I would stop.

I would turn around and shake my head at whoever it was trying to help me get in the door, whoever it was that was standing behind me ready to force me in the door if they had to, and they did have to many times. Mrs. Bishop, Mr. Pfaff, my mom, or sometimes all three. Sometimes, it included the principal or the counselor or the psychologist or anyone else who tried to help me. It was always really hard for me to separate from my mom when I was having these anxieties, and that was the first hurdle to be crossed every day. A lot of times, I refused to get out of the car once I got to school because I knew that meant she could leave me. By the time I had reached the door of my classroom, I was usually crying almost inconsolably and, if I could make out any words at all, they would probably be something along the lines of "I can't do it." Mr. Pfaff would tell me things like, "You got in the car this morning. You got out of the car. You made it all the way here to the door. The last step is to walk in." The whole morning was always such a feat that I was exhausted by the time I reached the door. Thinking back on all of the things I had just achieved to get there helped, but I was also facing each thing head on. Wherever I was at any given moment, whether it was the car, the fence leading into the school, or the door to my classroom, all I was thinking about was, "How do I get out of here?" And that is what was so tough to deal with for me. I wanted to be normal. I wanted to go to school without any problems. I wanted to walk through that door without a care in the world. But, at the same time, I wanted nothing more than to escape from it all. There was what seemed to be a rational side of my mind, and there was an irrational side of my mind in an intense battle with each other every single morning and the rational side hardly ever won.

Chapter Ten: French Fry Feelings

If it doesn't work, you haven't found the right strategy yet. Don't get too discouraged. We want to improve just as much as you want us to.

When my mom would leave me at school in the mornings, I would feel like I was now in a place where nobody understood me. She was the only person who really somewhat knew what I was feeling, who knew me better than anyone, and who was fighting so hard to make sure I was okay, and it was always a very hard separation. She was the person I felt the most comfortable confiding in, and I always felt like once she wasn't there anymore, I didn't have anybody. In elementary school, that really was somewhat the case. A lot of mornings, my dad was the one who dropped me off, and I had a hard time leaving the house knowing my mom was staying behind. Once I got to the school, I would have a hard time leaving my dad. Like I said, I had wonderful elementary school teachers who did the best they could and really did help me through a lot. But I was completely mainstreamed, and even though I was academically inclined, and I was technically able to be mainstreamed, there were a lot of other areas where I was struggling. I could have used more support than I got and it probably would have benefited me greatly. My teachers had a whole class of children who were just as important as I was and needed just as much attention as I did. They couldn't neglect all of them to help me, but I do think I would have had a better elementary school experience had I gotten a little bit more downtime. Those couple of times I went to Mrs. Marzolf's room were so helpful to me, and it would have been wonderful if I would have been entering campus everyday knowing I was going to have a time in the day for something like that. While my actual teachers couldn't necessarily provide that for me, it would have been nice if I would have had someone who could. That was probably the most difficult age for someone like me to be in a normal classroom all day, and that was the only age where that was required of me. Every year after that, I was granted that downtime.

Mrs. Bishop and Mr. Pfaff were the second closest I have ever been to being understood. At first, I was even a little bit of a mystery to them, but once they got to know me a little bit better, they began to see it too. While it was still very hard to get dropped off by my mom in middle school, it was also easier because I knew I was with people who were really trying to understand me and get me what I needed. My mom knew that too. She didn't like having to leave me at school if she didn't know who I was going to be with or what I was going to do. There was one morning in fifth grade when she pulled away in our old van, and I was standing on the curb crying. I had no intention of walking into my classroom late, and I didn't know what I was going to do. I probably would have just stood there crying until somebody came along to help me or until my class went out to recess. It had only been a few seconds and she came driving back down the road. She had been able to see me in her mirrors. I got back in the car and she took me to work with her, which happened more often than it didn't on my bad days in elementary school. Once I got to middle school, Mrs. Bishop or Mr. Pfaff would actually come out to the car and get me. She never had to just leave me in the parking lot like that. I had resource teachers who saw me for who I was. I was someone who needed that help, and they were going to give it to me, even if it was harder on them to do so. I didn't have any academic issues, I looked like I was completely fine, and I was a good student, but I had a lot more issues than people could see at first glance. And they cared to help not just me, but my whole family, through the good and the bad of a situation like ours.

The next school year, when I transitioned to seventh grade, Mr. Pfaff became the vice principal and a new resource teacher, Miss Proctor, came in. She ended up also being a great teacher for me in my seventh and eighth grade years. I was put into her Supported Studies class. It was a class for the resource kids to work on their homework at the very end of the day. If you didn't have any homework, you had to read a book. It became a great source of that downtime for me in middle school and high school (and I never had to do my homework at home!). Mrs. Bishop told me the story of Miss Proctor asking her questions about my disability. Mrs. Bishop told her I had autism and she replied that I didn't seem like I had any autistic qualities. Mrs. Bishop said, "Oh, she does once you get to know her!" And Miss Proctor definitely got to know me and she saw all of my autistic qualities. When Mrs. Bishop told me that story, I remember thinking about a time a couple of days earlier when I had been in my Supported Studies class. We all had school planners and Miss Proctor did a "planner check" every day to make sure we were being organized and keeping track of everything we needed to do. I remembered her checking my planner off and smiling at me when she did it. I think that maybe she and Mrs. Bishop had just had that conversation, and the reason she smiled is because I had every birthday and/or important date written out in my planner along with all of my homework assignments. There was another time one of the aides was checking our planners, and she came up behind me as I was writing in it. I didn't have anything else to do, so I was just writing out birthdays and important dates for weeks in advance. The aide asked me, "Why are you just barely writing everything out?" After I realized she was talking to me, I flipped back a few pages to the week we were actually in. She said, "Wow. You're really planning ahead." The autistic qualities aren't always visible on the surface. For me, it is in the little things that I do and the quirky ways I live my life. You just have to know what to look for and my middle school teachers definitely knew what they were seeing when they looked at me. I was accepted and it was the first time I had found myself feeling safe in a school environment, even though I still had all of my anxieties.

There were many reasons pondered as to why I was having all of the trouble I had in sixth grade. A lot of strategies were tried out to attempt to get me back on the right track and help me through it. There were a lot of mornings that were just spent with Mrs. Bishop and Mr. Pfaff in their classrooms. Mrs. Bishop had a P.E. class she taught first thing in the morning and I would just go outside with them and observe whatever they were doing. One morning, they were playing Silent Ball and I decided to play with them. Every time that someone had to sit down, Mrs. Bishop would say something along the lines of, "Are you sad that you didn't catch the ball?" And if they said they weren't sad, then they had to do sit-ups. I remember preparing myself to answer that question and I was going to say I *was* sad (even though that was a lie) so that I didn't have to do sit-ups. Then, when I didn't catch the ball, she asked me, "Jillian, are you sad that you didn't catch the ball?" At that moment, I had forgotten I was going to lie, so I gave my honest answer, "No." She gasped, "No?!" And then I had to do sit-ups. I was never good at lying. Often times, my resource teachers have seen the potential in me a lot better than I am capable of seeing it in myself. They both had moments with me where they were like another set of parents; they would tell me when they knew that I could do better and they also understood when I needed more time. It is like Molly, my social learning therapist, will sometimes say in our monthly meetings, "This is tough love, Jill." And that is what I have received from them always. They have always succeeded at pushing me completely out of my comfort zone and, usually, I'm mad about it, but then I feel appreciative of it later.

The first day I met Mrs. Bishop, she told me she had a dance team she taught at school and she was wondering if I liked to dance. I actually did like to dance a little bit, and I had been a part of a dance company in a nearby town when I was in fourth grade. The routine I had learned there over the course of a year was a tap dance routine that only consisted of me and one other boy. We worked on it together for an entire year, and then it ended horribly. We got to the point where we had our recital, and when I got there, I was way too nervous to go out on the stage. My partner's sister had helped us learn the routine throughout the year, and she ended up performing it with him for me. That was my only dance experience, but somehow Mrs. Bishop convinced me to try out for her team. That is completely out of character for me, but I did it and I had a lot of fun. It was a color guard team. There were dance portions of the routine, but there were also flags and rifles that we turned and tossed and danced with. I didn't expect to make it on the team, but I did and there were two other girls with autism on the team as well. Mrs. Bishop is very inclusive and she took something that most people would have deemed as too hard to handle and she saw the potential in it. The day I found out that I made the team, I was so excited and I used my mom's phone to text Lindsey, who was living in Texas at the time. I made the mistake of not letting her know that it was me texting her so she sent back, "Wow. She must be a better dancer than we thought!"

Over the course of the next two years, I went to practice every Friday after school and, most days, I dreaded it. I always liked it once I was there, but in the midst of a rough morning, I couldn't help but think about the two extra hours I would have to live through that day. There were a few afternoons where we were in the middle of a run through and I just stopped and started crying. Sometimes, I would get frustrated with myself if I wasn't understanding how to do one of the moves, but I was also just in a very fragile state. Something that a lot of people might not know about autism is that there tends to be non-verbal tendencies in a completely verbal person, even though you might not think so. Lots of autistic people could probably tell you that despite the fact that they are verbal, there are times when they are unable to communicate verbally, especially during a meltdown. I didn't have the ability to say I needed a break or I was feeling stressed. Instead, I would begin to do what I thought I was supposed to be doing, but I was unable to ignore the pressing anxiety and I would start to cry. I think that being on the dance team was actually a really good thing for me though. Being a part of a team made me feel like I had a purpose, and I was involved in something in a way that I hadn't ever been before and I have never been since. I actually really enjoyed learning the routines and practicing them, and I made some friends with the other girls. However, performing was a different story.

We performed at the school basketball games, and we drove a couple of hours a few times a year to compete at a competition. Those were always really fun, yet very stressful days. I always cried for one reason or another right before we performed, and I think that all of the other girls on the team just kind of accepted that about me. Nobody ever really asked me what I was crying about. Most times, it was just because I was nervous, and it gave me a lot of anxiety to go out there and perform. When I am nervous like that, it seems as though all of my other senses get heightened. My sense of smell seems to almost get stronger, the lights seem to get brighter, noises become louder, and it is like everything else starts to get to me even more than it normally does. When I am nervous, I can't eat and if I try I will nearly make myself physically sick. I get in the situation fairly often where I am out to eat at a restaurant, and I get too nervous to eat all of my food. I almost always have to get a to-go box for practically my entire plate of food because of this. When I was at competitions for dance team, it was the same thing, but a little bit worse of a situation because of all of the different aspects thrown into it. First of all, I would already be on edge because it was a long day, and I wasn't able to do my rope or my music. That always made things very hard for me. Then, I was extremely nervous on top of that and I would be rehearsing the routine over and over again in my mind, which only drove me even more crazy. On top of *that*, I would be in a gym where there were fluorescent lights and a lot of people smashed into one space and, of course, tall bleachers. It was not a good mix, but it was all a very valuable experience for me and it was a lot of fun.

In the meantime, I was almost always having trouble during the school days, especially in the mornings at drop-off time. I did have a more secure environment I was entering into with Mr. Pfaff and Mrs. Bishop and that was very helpful, but it didn't take away all of my anxiety surrounding school. It was still very present and it took a lot of work, which seemed to me like hopeless work. They tried many different things to get me to feel more comfortable coming to school. They collectively decided I could get picked up at one o'clock just to have a shorter day. Either my dad or my grandparents would come to the school, and take me home for the remainder of the day. This didn't work out the way they thought it might. What they were trying to fix was the fact I never wanted to come to school. They figured that knowing I would have less time at school every day would make it easier for me to get there. I could see where they thought that because, at first, I had significantly less trouble coming to school on shorter days. However, after awhile, even knowing I had less time didn't change things for me. I was still having a lot of trouble getting to school. Therefore, when they tried giving me shorter days as a solution to the problem, it didn't work. The reason for that is that the length of the day wasn't necessarily the problem. It probably contributed to my anxiety in a way, but it wasn't the main issue causing all of this. That is when they knew they needed to do some more work, try out some more strategies, and figure out exactly what was causing me to have all of this trouble. Like I said, if it isn't working, then you haven't found the right strategy yet. It is very hard to try to identify a cause for all of these problems when there is such a big communication barrier. It probably almost seems impossible. What was hard about it for me was the fact that *I* didn't even know what was causing all of it myself. I wasn't going to ever be able to communicate what was wrong if I didn't even know what was wrong. That is where all of the trial and error comes in and nobody can do anything but guess. The length of the school day just ended up not being the main problem so we had to try something else.

There was also a point in time a little bit earlier in the year where they thought having time to do my rope while at school would help me. This was a good idea. Coming to school knowing that I was going to get some downtime had the potential of being very helpful to me. It would make for a great break from all of the hecticness I was experiencing during the school day. I brought my rope in my backpack, and after I ate lunch, I walked to Mrs. Bishop's room and she took me to a classroom that was off by itself in the corner of the school. All of the kids that were usually in that class were at lunch and the teachers were gone on their break, so it was the only room I would have completely to myself. She gave me a timer so I wouldn't get so wrapped up that I would keep doing my rope and end up late to class. I only did it for a few days and it was definitely helpful when I did. After a few days of doing that, the two teachers who used that classroom came back from their lunch break early and walked in when I was doing my rope. They knew I had been doing it sometimes during that time frame, but they didn't know I was in there right at that moment. I had luckily seen them through the window, so I put my rope back into my backpack and started to pick up my timer. But I know for a fact that, by the look on my face, I did not hide my terror. I was freaked out they almost saw me doing my rope. I was already at the point where it was very private, and I am so glad I was not too caught up in the moment to notice they were about to come into the room. They actually both played Rec League basketball with Ethan and Austin, and they had been around me in the Special Ed room on occasion, so they already knew that I was an anxious mess. They apologized to me and then they left to go yell at Mrs. Bishop. I had quite a bit of time left to do my rope, but I was so traumatized that I didn't want to. I packed up and left and then I ran into Mrs. Bishop just as I was turning the corner. She was on her way to see if I was okay and she goes, "They yelled at me." After that, I was a little bit too scared to do my rope at school anymore.

Once I got further into the school year, I think they began to realize the transition was the hardest part of the morning. It was true that once I got into my English class (on the occasion that I did), it was basically over. I would have a few minutes of crying and then I would sit down at my desk and I would be okay. The biggest hurdle to cross was just simply getting into the classroom. The other kids in my English class were really kind to me, and they tried to make me feel comfortable. I had a friend, Eli, who was exceptionally kind-hearted when it came to me having trouble. She would actually stand outside the classroom with me and try to make me feel better, so that I would eventually come inside. It was harder for me in some ways because I knew she didn't quite know the details of my situation, but she actually gave me that push I needed without even realizing she was doing it. Eventually, they decided to try basically forcing me into the classroom. They would walk me up to the door, and once I got in, they would shut it and walk away. When I was that young, I never really tried to follow them. I did chase my mom through the halls of the high school once I got older, but in sixth grade, I don't remember doing that. I think a lot of it was knowing, in the back of my mind, that I was safe. Mrs. Bishop, Mr. Pfaff, and Miss Proctor were safe people for me, and even when my mom was gone, I knew I had somebody. In the beginning of high school, there were times where I didn't have that support or that sense of safety, so my mom leaving me was even more difficult. But all through middle school, I did have that support, and I knew that I was safe without my mom. I remember as soon as the door was shut, I started to cry and a bunch of kids came up to make sure I was okay. My teacher, Mrs. Pettit, was very patient with me and the anxiety I had surrounding school didn't have anything to do with her as a teacher, the kids as my peers, or the class in general. Nobody knew what was wrong and they didn't have to be as supportive as they were, but it made a world of a difference to me that they did.

Soon, I tried my own strategies to make it so I *didn't* have to go to school. I hid the keys to my mom's car before we left the house so we couldn't leave. The bad thing was that after she dropped me off, she had to go to work and I almost always made her late regardless. On this particular week, my cousin Blake was graduating from high school and most everybody in my family was going, but Lindsey and Teddy were going to take me to the county fair instead. I have always loved the fair because it feels so hometown-y and I LOVE the rides. Teddy and Lindsey just waited for me as I got on ride after ride after ride. I think I rode one of them at least twenty times in a row. I just couldn't get enough. However, I was earning the chance to go to the fair and that was the week that I hid the car keys. I thought it was kind of funny, but everyone else, not so much. I still ended up getting to go to the fair because it hadn't been as horrible of a week as it usually was. However, I did miss out on the privilege to go to one of my school dances I really wanted to go to because I had so much trouble the week leading up to it. I remember being pretty upset about that because I knew I wasn't intentionally having trouble going to school. I didn't know exactly what was causing me all of my trouble, but I knew I wasn't doing it on purpose. I know it sounds crazy, but every time I get in a situation where I am upset or nervous, I start to lose control. I have never, ever wanted to have a meltdown or experience my barrier. I have always felt like it is my mind that decides it for me. I can think about how bad I don't want to get upset all I want, but if it is going to happen, it will happen. It doesn't matter what I want, where I'm at, or who I'm with. My autism will take over. Not allowing me to go to the dance was kind of a last resort to see if I would change my ways in order to get to do something I wanted to do, but that didn't work simply because I truly was not doing this on purpose.

There were other times where I would do everything I possibly could not to get into the car in the morning. I would stall or I would run. I would throw things or I would hit things. There was one morning where Lindsey was home visiting and she said, "This is scary." I'm sure it was a little bit scary from an outside perspective, but I didn't want to be seen that way. I was very anxious and I was trapped in a mind that was not going to give me a break from all of the anxieties and the fear. My eighth grade year, my mom and I were driving on the highway on our way to the school, and I had my hand on the door handle threatening to jump out of the car. She just kept saying, "No. You are not going to jump out of the car." When we got to the school, she told Mr. Pfaff what I tried to do and he said, "Do you want to break your arms and your legs?" At the time, I didn't even fathom how hurt I would get by jumping out of a moving car in the middle of the highway because that wasn't what I was trying to do. I know now I definitely would have regretted that decision, but I wasn't threatening to jump out because I wanted to hurt myself. I was just really terrified to go to school, and I didn't want to even get there because I knew that I would have to stay.

On the last day of my sixth grade year, we had an assembly in the gym and when it was over, everybody cried. Literally, I think every single girl in the building cried, except for me. I just looked around and thought, "What is going on?! You guys are sad?!" This happened on the last day of school all three years I was in middle school. Even on the last day of my eighth grade year, I didn't cry and I really tried to that time. I knew I wasn't going to have my resource teachers I had grown to love, and I willed myself to think about them so I could cry too. But that didn't work. Going to school? I am a crying mess. The last day? Crying was impossible. I remember my dad picking me up on my last day of sixth grade. For my whole life, he has always said, "Guess what today is?" I will say, "The last day of school!" And he'll go, "Nope. It's the last day of school!" We drove away and I didn't even think about school until August.

Two days before school started up my seventh grade year, I told my mom I wasn't ready to go back. That isn't a very good thing to hear when you are just about to embark on another full school year. And at first, I did have a little bit of trouble. Mrs. Bishop's first period of the day was a prep period some of the time, but she warned me that there were going to be times where she would be testing students, and I was not going to be allowed in her room when that was going on. Mr. Pfaff had changed over to the vice principal, so he was also busier with more responsibilities and people to deal with than he had the previous year. He also wasn't just in one spot. He had an office, but I was never completely certain he would be in there if I looked for him. Miss Proctor had luckily started working at my school, and that gave us an extra person to go to if we needed it. However, these were difficult changes for me to come to terms with. I knew they were always there if I needed them, but I was worried I wouldn't have them at the times I would need them the most, which was typically the first thing in the morning. However, Mr. Pfaff and Mrs. Bishop decided to make a few changes to my schedule once the school year started to help me out a little bit and it really, really worked.

There were two lunch periods at my school and they were based off of the grade we were in. I was in the second lunch period of the day, but they decided to also put me in the first lunch period. During first lunch, I was an aide for another girl who had autism. We were quite different from each other. She was not as mainstreamed as I was, but over the course of the year, I saw a lot of similarities between the two of us. For example, I always feel my french fries before I eat them. I'm not exactly sure why, but I think it has something to do with the texture. I prefer soft fries over crispy fries, and I think that I like to feel them to see if it is the right texture for me to eat it or not. I actually still do that whenever I eat any type of finger food, which is very often. It drives my mom nuts because I will either only eat the soft part, or I will crumple my food into pieces when I feel it. One day, I was watching the girl I had lunch with while she was eating across from me and I said, "You feel your french fries like I do." She looked at me and went, "What are you talking about?" She didn't quite understand it the way I did, and I would have never even noticed that I did it had my mom not always gotten on me about it. It is just one of those weird quirks that never really gets explained, and I wouldn't have ever attributed it to my autism had I not seen her do it also.

There were some other things this girl did that I recognized as those little quirks and that were similar to things I did or could see myself doing. There was a time where there was a "Code Red" drill in the middle of first lunch. This is an unusual time for those kinds of things to happen, and there had actually been a real Code Red when I was in fourth grade, so I didn't think it was a drill. I went running and I was just yelling behind me to her, "Come on! Get in the closet!" A bunch of kids packed into the closet in the gym, which was attached to the cafeteria, and then I realized she wasn't with me. I was worried about her the whole time because I still thought the drill was real. I even purposely stood by the big bin of basketballs just in case I had to start throwing them. After the Code Red was over and I figured out it was just a practice drill, I found her and asked her where she had been that whole time. She had gone to the trash can in the cafeteria, and she had been throwing her food away before she had gone into a different closet with a different set of kids. At my school, there were certain trash cans for certain foods and you sorted your trash as you threw it away. You put your fruit in one trash bin, everything else in the other, and then you stacked your empty trays on the table. While I was panicking, she had been sorting out her food and going through her normal routine of throwing her food away. I had just left all of my stuff on the table and ran. It made a lot of sense to me though. Throwing her plate of food away before she left the cafeteria was part of her routine, and she was less capable of breaking that than I was. I tried to explain to her that sometimes in a situation like that, it might be better to just leave your plate on the table, but she didn't like that idea very much. And, after that, Mr. Pfaff always warned me when there was going to be a Code Red so I wouldn't think it was real.

Being able to have both first and second lunch was a great thing for more than one reason. First of all, it gave me a great experience to be able to meet another girl who had autism and connect with her. She became one of my friends that year, and it meant a lot to me to be able to be that for her as well. She is an amazing girl, and I absolutely loved being able to sort of be a mentor for someone like her. It was also very special to me to be able to see our similarities and I think it actually taught me a lot about autism. I know that there are so many differences amongst every autistic person and everyone is affected in such different ways. There are no two people with autism who are exactly alike and struggle with all the same things. But I really do believe there is a connection between all of us, no matter what our struggles are. We are the only people who truly know what it is like to go through life on the spectrum.

Everyone experiences autism differently and my autism is vastly different than what some other autistic people will experience. However, I really do feel if you were to hear the stories of every person on the autism spectrum, you would see similarities between all of them. It might be in the little things that seem to just be weird quirks, such as feeling your french fries before you eat them, or it might be in the big things, such as not quite understanding the art of forming and maintaining friendships. I have a hard time with that and I also feel my french fries before I eat them. My friend was a different person with different struggles who also had a hard time forming and maintaining friendships and she felt her french fries before she ate them. We fell on different parts of the spectrum, we had our differences in what we struggled with, but I began to see those similarities as I got to know her. I think I would slowly start to see them if I got to know any other autistic person closely over the course of a year. There are a lot of huge differences, but I do really believe there is a general understanding of autism that we all share because we are the people who know and live with autism.

In terms of how I did with school, having both lunch periods made my life so much better. My seventh grade year was my best year in middle school by a landslide. A huge, huge landslide. Having both lunch periods gave me the opportunity to have that downtime. I was away from the stresses of a classroom. I didn't feel like I had to constantly be doing my rope in my head and that was because I was simply relaxed. I was just able to sit with my friend while she ate her lunch and then go outside. We would sometimes just sit on a bench and chat. We would talk to one of the autism aides, Mrs. Gomez, and we would sometimes hang out with some of the other kids. We would occasionally play catch with a ball or do something along those lines, but most of the time, we just walked around and talked. Then, when second lunch came along, she would go to class, and I would go back to the cafeteria and actually eat my lunch. Then, I would have more opportunities to talk and relax with other people I called my friends. My anxiety basically went back to being completely situational. I had bad mornings when I had my feelings hurt or when I was anxious about something, but I didn't have the chronic anxiety towards school. I would say that this was because I knew that I was going to get a little bit of a break. It truly made a huge difference for me.

Chapter Eleven: Hockey Puck

Just because you can't see it doesn't mean it isn't there. We have to adapt everyday and sometimes we also need to be adapted for.

Halfway through my seventh grade year, my schedule changed again. Two of my classes switched with each other and I ended up with an opening for my first period of the day. We had to figure out where to put me for that period. One time, I told Mrs. Bishop, "You guys overestimate my abilities." In other words, I was saying that they were asking too much of me and there were things they were expecting me to do that I just felt like I really couldn't do. She goes, "I will always overestimate your abilities!" Now, I would say it probably isn't really overestimating, but rather it is seeing my full potential, which I haven't always been capable of seeing, and helping me reach it. Unfortunately, reaching it almost always means getting pushed out of your comfort zone one way or another. My mom attended a meeting for me that discussed the change in my schedule and she decided to keep this information from me until Christmas break. She didn't want it to throw me off and she thought giving me time to process it while I was at home would be better. The class they were going to be giving me was office aiding. She knew that would be hard for me and, if that was the case, it was going to be hard for her, too.

One of my greatest fears was still walking into one of my classes late. When I had all of my trouble in sixth grade, having to walk in late only added to my anxiety. I was almost always late in sixth grade because I was having so many meltdowns, and I was trying to stay away from school for as long as I possibly could every single morning. The reason walking in late scared me was because I knew everyone would turn around and look at me. When I had a rough morning, and I had been crying a lot, the last thing I wanted was that kind of attention from my peers. I just wanted to go unnoticed and I would have gladly suffered the consequences of not going into class at all if it meant that I didn't have to walk in late. Being an office aide would entail walking into a full classroom over and over again for an hour every single day. I had to run slips to all of the classes, and I had to talk to anybody (mainly parents) who came up to the window of the front office. Those were both going to be really hard things for me to do and I was mortified. All I could think about were all of the things that could possibly happen. It had only been a few weeks since Mr. Pfaff had walked me to my first period class a little bit late, and I walked in only for another kid to be in my chair. The odds seem very slim, but this actually happened to me a total of three times in my entire school career. I hadn't known what to do, but my teacher ended up getting another chair for me to sit in. However, those were the kind of things that made it scary for me to think about office aiding. There were so many bad things that could happen.

I actually ended up office aiding for the remainder of my seventh grade year, my entire eighth grade year, and two more years once I got to high school. I loved it and it was a great experience for me (and also another good form of a break), but I did have my mishaps throughout it. Sometimes, the classroom doors were locked, and I didn't want to knock because that drew too much attention to me. The other girl I office aided with told me that she just knocked (she made it sound so easy!), and I would always bring the slip back to her if the door was locked because I just couldn't do it. Before I started doing that, I would just put it in the next box for the second period office aides to deal with. That wasn't a good idea because, usually, the slips were urgent and the classes obviously changed. That person wasn't going to be with the same teacher during the next period. I caused all that confusion for the next people just because I was afraid to knock on the door! Occasionally, my barrier is present in more ways than just in my meltdowns. Sometimes, I have it in normal situations like that, too. It is whenever my anxiety just completely takes over and stops me from doing whatever it is I am trying to do. I almost always want to do it or wish I could, but it truly feels like I can't.

Another mishap I made was walking into the wrong room once. I figured it out right after I walked in and everyone turned around. (Awkward!) Sometimes, kids would ask me questions while I was in their room, such as "Who is the slip for?", and they would all listen eagerly to see if the slip was for them. That always threw me off when it happened because then I would have to look down at the paper in my hand and read the name that was on it when all I was supposed to be doing was handing it to the teacher. Once, a kid even pushed his chair back when I was walking by, which made me trip over him and then he laughed. There were also just some classrooms both in middle school and high school that I was more scared of than others. I was the most comfortable walking into a few certain rooms, and I tried to figure out why once I got to high school. I finally realized it was a lot harder for me to walk into rooms set up in such a way that I had to walk through all of the kids to get to the teacher. And, a lot of times, the desks were close together and I couldn't always count on people to make it easy for me to maneuver my way through them. (Like I said, I am very clumsy!) However, once seventh grade came to a close, I was a lot more comfortable walking into classrooms. I still did not like it if I was crying or having a meltdown, but I knew I could do it if I had to. It was no longer a problem in the mornings. Sometimes, it had been one even when I wasn't crying because having to walk in late would make me *start* crying. However, office aiding slowly helped fix all of that for me. I was pushed completely out of my comfort zone, but that is what helped me overcome that hurdle.

My eighth grade year was the worst year I ever had in terms of not wanting to go to school. I still had an incredible support system, but I was plagued with anxiety. Seventh grade was amazing and then it was like a switch flipped unexplainably. I went to school good for the first five days. That was pretty much it. I remember sitting in my science class on Friday of the first week and just having the inclination this was not going to be good. I could feel it. In April, I remember telling my cousin Melissa I had just gotten through a whole week without any bad mornings. It seriously took me until April to be able to say that. Having so many bad mornings one after the other really started to affect me in a lot of ways. My cousin's wife had a baby shower just a few weeks into the school year, and I had to tell my mom, "Go without me. I can't do it today." I have said before that family parties have a tendency to make me nervous. However, there have only been two times where I really didn't feel like I could muster up enough courage to go, and they were both when I was in eighth grade. I was just too tired from having to muster up a bunch of courage all five days in the week to go to school, and there were some weeks where I really didn't feel like I could add another thing to it. There were even some weekends where I basically slept the whole way through because I was emotionally exhausted.

When I transitioned to eighth grade, there were some changes that were difficult to adjust to, but the support I received remained the same. Mrs. Bishop announced at one of our dance team practices in the spring of my seventh grade year that she was pregnant. Her baby was due in the fall, and she didn't know if she was going to be able to have dance team the following year. As far as I knew, that was all of the change that was going to occur. Then, in July, my mom and I met up with her for lunch and she told us that she had found a new job. She had been commuting and she decided she wanted to work where she could be closer to her kids. Even though she left, she has always stayed in contact with us. I don't consider any of them just my teachers anymore. They are my teacher friends. All through high school, I sent them updates about things going on at school because, even though they couldn't be that involved, they could give me advice personally. I still had Mr. Pfaff at school with me in eighth grade, and I got to know Miss Proctor a lot better as well. She became a huge advocate for me when I didn't have Mrs. Bishop anymore, and she spent a lot of time working on getting me what I needed. Mr. Pfaff and Miss Proctor have also both moved on to new jobs since then and it was truly a gift from God that I was in middle school during the years the three of them were there. I can honestly tell you I would probably not have made it through school if I had not had the immense and unwavering support I received while I was there. And, on September 25th, when I got a text that said, "It's a girl!"

with a picture of a new baby, I actually felt important to somebody who wasn't a part of my family. But, in my heart, they are a part of my family and they are a huge part of my life.

I office aided the first period of the day again in eighth grade, which was a really good thing, because when I missed it due to a bad morning, I didn't fall behind in any work. I office aided with two really sweet and patient peers of mine, Alexandrea and Ricardo, who saw me crying a lot! In middle school, I was subjected to a lot of that, especially in eighth grade. My peers saw me crying all the time. Almost every single day, there was an incident that was embarrassing for me to think about later, but in the heat of the moment, I wasn't thinking about the people around me. My mindset was normally about getting out of wherever I was right at that moment. I wasn't worried about the other kids or what they were thinking about me. Later, I would have time to be humiliated that they had seen me in my meltdown state. In high school, it was even worse. Eventually, I kind of stopped seeing them. I didn't even notice them because my anxiety just completely took over. One time, my whole English class walked by me on their way to the library standing outside with my mom, both principals, and my high school resource teacher, Mr. Texara. I didn't want that at all. It was absolutely humiliating. I wanted to be accepted by them, yet they saw me in positions like that. I began to think that I was crazy because I knew that had to be what they all thought. But eventually, I just had to tell myself that none of those kids knew what I was going through, and they probably hardly gave it a second thought. I knew being outside with a bunch of adults like that was what I had to do because of the situation I was in. There was nothing I could do about it and I couldn't control what my peers thought about me. I just had to focus on getting better. There wasn't any time to worry about the stares or the thoughts behind them. If I could just eventually get to the point where I didn't have all of this anxiety anymore, I subsequently wouldn't have the stares anymore. I just wanted to try to get there.

After a couple of months of having a horrible time in eighth grade, I started to kind of realize where some of my anxiety was stemming from. This was different from my sixth grade year. I was able to pinpoint why I was having the amount of trouble I was having. After my office aiding class the first period of the day, I had my P.E. class. Then, I had another little break as an aide for one of the classes Miss Proctor taught.

This got put into place about two weeks into the school year. I had originally had a different class that period, but there were some people in there giving me a hard time, so they decided to move me out. Miss Proctor's class was one I really enjoyed, but I started to realize, even when I did make it to office aiding, I still felt plagued by my anxiety. I didn't stop feeling that way until I was in Miss Proctor's class, which was after office aiding and after P.E. I have stated previously that I am a very uncoordinated person. I already knew that about myself and I knew that I didn't enjoy P.E. But it was a little bit more complicated than just not liking it, and that has been something that I have had a hard time getting people to understand. That most certainly had something to do with it. I *didn't* like P.E. But why didn't I like P.E.? That is the question. I didn't like P.E. because I was being expected to do things that were nearly impossible for someone like me to do. Physically impossible? No. Mentally impossible? Pretty much.

It was absolutely torturous for me to be in the middle of a group of girls who were screaming and shoving and kicking their legs and all going after the same object. It almost puts me into fight or flight mode just thinking about it. It almost makes me want to cry thinking about being forced to run through a group of girls who are all trying to throw a ball at me to get me "out." And while everyone else is staring at me, no less. Those things were terrifying for me. My family can tell you I am actually good at shooting a basketball and making it into the net. Would I ever be able to do that if I had a bunch of screaming girls waving their hands in my face? Absolutely not. And I was being told over and over again by numerous people to "Try harder," "Get in there", and "Catch the ball!!!" (I can still hear that girl's voice in my head yelling at me). None of the people who said those things to me were autistic. None of them could even begin to understand what it's like, yet they took it upon themselves to make it one thousand times harder than it needed to be for *me*. I was having my barrier constantly when I was in that class. I knew what was expected of me. I didn't need to keep being told. I didn't want to participate in the games in the first place. That is true, but I knew that I had to. As a result, I wanted to be able to at least avoid making everyone mad at me, and that was kind of unavoidable because I couldn't do what they were expecting of me. That alone seemed to make some of the other girls in my class mad at me. It felt like I was getting personally insulted every time someone said something to me about it. It felt like that because my barrier was there. Everyone was yelling at me because I had a barrier in my mind they couldn't see, but I could feel with every inch of me. That makes it feel like they were yelling at me because of my autism. Even though I know that was never what any of them would have wanted to do, and a lot of them didn't even know I was autistic, it *was* how it made me feel because I knew that my barrier was there due to my autism. If I wasn't autistic, I wouldn't have had that kind of trouble with the games. I might not have liked them, but I would not have felt like I was being forced to do something that I really did not feel like I could do and that was what was happening to me constantly in my P.E. class.

There was a time where one of the girls was standing in front of me kind of taunting me. We were playing a game and she was standing on my side of the line, which meant that I was supposed to tag her, and she was just standing there waiting for me to do it. I would have done it, but she was also hurting my feelings because of the way she was taunting me. In addition, everyone else was watching because she was like, "Tag me. Are you going to tag me?" Because I knew she was just making fun of me, and also because everyone else was watching me, I had my barrier in my mind. I knew that everyone was waiting for me to tag her, but I just couldn't do it. There were a million thoughts running through my mind, and I was getting more overwhelmed with every second that passed. Then, another girl came up and yelled at me, "Oh my gosh. Just tag her!" I started to move towards her because I felt even more under pressure now than I had a couple seconds before and then my barrier stopped me. I froze. She yelled at me again, "Just tag her!" And I just repeated the same thing over again. Then, she went running after the girl herself, the girl screamed, and then ran back over the line. They both might as well have just slapped me right across the face. I don't know what the point of that whole ordeal was. They didn't know what they were putting me through in my mind when they did that, but it threw me into a complete meltdown and I fell apart just standing right there. They didn't even look at me after I started to cry, and I had to sit out the rest of the game that day.

There was another time where we were playing hockey in the gym. There were four teams and we were taking turns playing. At this particular moment, I was on the bleachers. The puck came up near me so everyone was waiting for me to throw it back into the game. For some reason, doing that made me nervous, and people looking at me made me nervous, so I went to hand it to the girl sitting next to me. She got this insulted look on her face, and she just slapped the hockey puck right out of my hand. People laughed, but I didn't think it was very funny. She had hit me, first of all, and she had done that because I was nervous and I was nervous because I had my barrier. I had a whole meltdown again that day, and I just moved to where my teacher was sitting, but I was unable to verbally explain to her what happened because I was having a meltdown. Every time I had a meltdown like that, it affected me for days. And in this class, it seemed like I was battling people who were against me because of my disability, even if they didn't know that or mean to be doing it. I also didn't have any allies. We played flag football for two complete weeks and I had two other girls on my team. One of them threw the ball to me during the very first play and I didn't catch it. That was the only time I got it thrown to me for the whole two weeks. They would look at me sometimes, hesitate, and then decide it wasn't worth it. That was nice, in a way, because I wasn't worried about having to catch the ball, and nobody was going to be mad at me when I *didn't* catch the ball. However, it still hurt my feelings because it really showed me I was just seen as inadequate. It wasn't even worth it to give me a simple chance to catch the ball and that was hurtful.

That P.E. class has had lasting effects on me. I didn't really have any friends in that class, which made it a little bit more difficult and lonely. I cried almost every time I walked through the door. Sometimes, I got to sit out because I was crying so hard. That was great. I didn't quite like how I had to get to that point, though. The girls who were in there with me were sweet girls and they didn't do anything wrong, but I was very negatively affected by just having been in that class. I got asked once by one of the girls why I sometimes didn't have to participate in the games. I just said, "I have a lot of anxiety." She was satisfied with that answer, and I was actually honored that she cared enough to ask. Other than that, I had a bad taste in my mouth with all of those girls. I know that it is unfair because there were some of them who never did anything hurtful to me. I also understand that the ones who did were young teenagers at the time they did those things, and they probably would never do them now. I had the opportunity to work really closely with one of them during my senior year and I was so upset by it at first. I just had her associated with my eighth grade P.E. class in my head, and I didn't like her simply because she had been in that class with me. After I got to know her, I ended up really liking her. She was a very nice girl, and that was when I realized that the feelings I had towards all of those people weren't really necessary. I had been going through a really, really tough time, but they didn't know the whole story and they didn't know just how deeply they were affecting me. However, it was still a horrible memory, and it was the main source of all of that anxiety my eighth grade year.

After the incident with the hockey puck, I was allowed to sit out for the rest of that two week unit. I didn't have to participate in hockey. I still dressed out in my P.E. clothes and did our daily warm-up, but then I got to just sit on the bleachers and watch the other girls play the game. On Wednesdays, there was no game. It was just a workout day. Everyone did their own thing and left everyone else alone. Wednesdays were wonderful, but every other day of the week was a huge struggle for me. It wasn't the actual idea of P.E. that was bothering me. It was specifically the games. I did significantly better going to school knowing I wasn't going to be forced to participate. I remember telling Miss Proctor, "See how much happier I am when I don't have to play hockey?" She told me that, yes, she could tell I was happier, but that was the problem. I think people thought that hockey itself had been the root of my anxiety and it was more situational than it was chronic. They figured I could just sit out this unit and then start back up again when the next one started. We were nearly halfway through the school year at this point and I was just starting to figure out it was P.E. that was causing me so much stress. I was sitting in Mr. Pfaff's office one morning. I hadn't gone to P.E and I was telling him that I didn't want to have to participate in the games. He said, "You don't have to. You already don't have to play hockey." I said, "No. I mean I don't want to do it all. I never want to do it again." That was the only time I've ever seen him not know what to say. He was probably like, "Oh my gosh. It's only November! This is going to be the longest year ever!" This was also pretty much the first time I had really been able to voice what my problem was. I was certain P.E. was the source of all of my anxiety, and I was putting my foot down by saying I wasn't going to do it anymore, but I didn't really have a choice.

Occasionally, I didn't make it to P.E. They always tried to get me there, but there were some days that it just wasn't going to happen. To other people, it might seem like I was just being given special treatment. It wasn't special attention or special treatment. It was me getting the help I needed. Making it to class was sometimes impossible and I mean that. They tried every single morning, but sometimes it was just too much. My eighth, ninth, and tenth grade years were the worst in terms of my anxiety. I think back on those years and I really think I had lost my mind. I wasn't myself at all. It was like an out of body experience for three years. I was mad, angry, and bitter at the world. I did a lot of things I felt bad for later, and I was on edge constantly. I have voiced all of that to Molly since then and she told me, "You weren't crazy. You were just really anxious and you didn't know how to handle it." I felt really alone, especially once I got to high school and all of the help I received was gone. The fact that I sometimes wasn't able to make it to P.E. was not a reflection onto the help I was receiving. I had a disability that was hindering my success and that is a fact. The only way that I was going to at least succeed a little bit was if I had that extra support. I needed to have a place to fall back on if, for whatever reason, P.E. was going to be too much for me to handle that day.

After that initial conversation in Mr. Pfaff's office, my entire school year was very bad. There was one day that I was crying very hard and it wasn't just a normal bad morning. It hadn't gotten to the point where it was a terrible morning. There had been one time back in sixth grade where Mrs. Bishop and Mr. Pfaff couldn't get me to calm down, and they had just called my mom to take me home for the day. This was a morning like that. I couldn't stop crying. I had already made it to class and then I had started back up again. This also happened a few times, but not very often. My teacher was standing outside with me trying to get me to come inside. We were standing out of view of the other kids who were all in the classroom, but then my teacher had me stand in front of the door. They all turned around and stared at me as I stood there crying. My teacher said to me, "They all need to see you like this." I think it was an attempt to humiliate it out of me, but the fact of the matter is that is impossible. The reason anyone would even think that could be possible was because they had the wrong perception of what my issues were. It wasn't something I could be humiliated out of. I had already experienced a lot of humiliation because of my disability and that had never made any of this go away. I cannot stress enough that I wasn't crying everyday just because I wanted to. I actually wanted to do the opposite. A lot of times, it was thought of as a matter of disobedience. Typically, I felt like a huge burden on my teachers and the people who were trying to help me, but I didn't want to be that way. Knowing some people looked at my situation and had that perception only made me feel a lot worse. I was trapped in a mind full of anxieties and I didn't know how to put it into words. The only thing that I could do was cry and that was unacceptable and misunderstood to some people.

On the last day of school, I was having a conversation with one of my teachers, and they jokingly said something along the lines of me pulling the "autey card" when I got to high school. The word "autey" was obviously in reference to my autism. I truly don't think it was meant in a serious way, but the way it could potentially come across is what makes being understood as an autistic person even more difficult. It could be seen as saying that I used my autism as an excuse to get out of things or to get what I wanted. I think both the idea that I use my autism as an excuse, and the idea that I am being disobedient are the two biggest misconceptions I have had with people over the years. Throughout my years of school, I had so many wonderful teachers who were very accommodating to me. However, there was sometimes a lack of understanding of my autism that made it difficult to get what I needed.

After I wrote my first paper in sixth grade explaining how I felt, I wrote a paper at the beginning of every school year to help my teachers understand me a little bit better. Most of them did their absolute best to help me succeed in their class, but there were a few who didn't understand my autism because of the way I look and appear on the outside. That isn't necessarily their fault because if you don't have a complete understanding of what autism is, then it *is* something that can be confusing. I was never a problem in the classroom in terms of instruction. I sat there quietly, I did my work, and I didn't struggle with academics, for the most part. I understand it can be hard to look at a student like me and wonder why I need any accomodations at all, but I care to be successful as a student, and I won't be if I am not getting the help I need. Therefore, the fact that some teachers didn't understand my autism had the ability to be detrimental to my success in school. I just recently sent one of my college professors an email regarding my autism and she replied with, "What does that mean? Can you elaborate for me?" When I read it, I figured she had never really been around it before, and she didn't have a clear understanding of it. Autism can be a very hard thing for people to grasp. I sent her back an email that basically told her why a three-hour-long college class would be hard for me and she said, "Thank you for letting me know. I just wanted to make sure we were on the same page in order to move forward." To me, this was wonderful because I had a teacher who cared enough to make sure that she understood what I needed in order to help me succeed in her class.

At my annual IEP meeting my freshman year, it was pondered by a couple of the adults working with me that maybe I should have to walk home every time I had a bad morning. We told them I lived too far away from the school, and they said, "Well, how about she has to ride the bus home?" It would have been giving me a consequence for something I really couldn't help and that has stuck with me. I was having the problems I was having because I was autistic, so it felt like I would have been receiving a punishment for just simply being autistic. I can't help that I have autism as much as I can't help that my hair is blonde. I could dye it if I wanted to. I could try to camouflage it, but the reality is that this is how I was born. And if you are going to work with kids like me, you have to understand that the battle is in the mind. The barrier that I experience feels very real to me. It stops me from completing simple tasks as soon as the smallest amount of anxiety creeps in, and it can take years to accomplish something that my barrier is standing in the way of. That is a lot of what I am battling in those moments when I am upset. I'm not just upset for no reason. It is just barrier after barrier after barrier. There is also always the intense need to do my rope and my music. When I went to school, I had to stifle those feelings all day long. It was exhausting to get through the day, and when I started out on a bad note, the feeling was even stronger because I was more on edge. Those were the things I was dealing with on those bad mornings, but once I stepped foot onto campus, the battle was no longer just inside of me. Everyone around me was involved. Everyone who looked at me, everyone who made unwarranted and insensitive comments, everyone who didn't want to give me the help, and everyone who thought I deserved a consequence for what I was going through. They were now half the battle and the other half still fought on within my mind. The lack of understanding in terms of autism is huge. People don't know what it is and that causes a lot of problems for the people who are affected by it daily. The least you can do is be compassionate.

I am going to run into a lot of people who are completely oblivious to the things I deal with because of my autism. That isn't a big deal, but there are going to be some people who truly don't believe me. To me, that *is* a big deal. I had someone accuse me of lying once. She said to me, "I think that boy over there has autistics." I said, "I have that. I have *autism*." She goes, "What do you do?" She was meaning in terms of stimming, which would be my rope and my music. I was immediately embarrassed at that question, and I said to her, "I don't know." I was only in seventh grade at the time, so my autism was still very much a secret, and I didn't want to tell her about my rope and my music. She said to me, "Well, if you don't know, then you don't have it." It was kind of funny because she wasn't even referring to it in the right way, but the times I have felt as though people weren't completely convinced I was really someone who needed the help I was getting were not so comical to me. I have never pulled an "autey" card. I was never just given special treatment for the fun of it. If we were thinking in terms of fun, I would have come to school without crying every day. That would have been grand, but the situation I was in required help and a little bit of extra work. Even though it came with a lot of hardships, I really needed the help.

Chapter Twelve: Knight In Shining Armor

It always depends on every aspect of the situation. If it works once, it might not work the next time.

When I transitioned to high school, I was in for it. I didn't even know what was coming. I had many opportunities for learning and growth, and I did a lot of both, but I had a lot of hard times right in the beginning. I had a lot of hurdles to jump over. I was dealing with a lot of misunderstandings, and I was kind of losing touch with myself and reality. My rope and my music are amazing tools and I love to stim in the ways that I do, but it can be very hard to regulate them. They are a coping mechanism, but they have a lot of power over me. When I got to high school, I thought I was losing my mind. When I think back on the beginning of high school, I honestly still think that I did lose my mind. People close to me have disputed these claims, but it was the closest I have ever been to really falling to pieces in the midst of all of the things that I have dealt with my whole life. I was doing my rope and my music probably too much and I was getting consumed with that need to stim. I was depending on it more than I ever have. Sometimes, I think that people with autism can seem like they are not taking things in. Then, it might shock you when they recite the whole periodic table, or repeat back to you everything that you said word for word a few weeks ago. I have been around children who are kind of like this. They are taking in so much more than you realize. There were times where teachers didn't think I was listening to them during class. In my case, I would attribute this to my "rope world."

For me, it is called a rope world. To the rest of the world, it doesn't really have a name, but it is a world in which autistic people go to in their mind. It varies for everyone and I cannot speak for every autistic person, but it was incredibly easy for me to get stuck in that world. My mom never wanted to let that happen to me. During the summer, I had a lot more time to do my rope and my music, and I took advantage of every spare minute I had to do so. However, when it started to happen too much, she would take me out on a drive or offer to play a board game with me. It is important for me to take a break from my rope and my music every once in a while, even though they are really good for me. In reality, I am stimming almost constantly. When I am cleaning up at work, I am usually stimming in my head to get myself through that. When I am watching a show on T.V., I am stimming to it. Typically, I don't go more than a couple hours without doing some form of stimming. It is healthy for me to be able to separate from that, but there have been times in my life where I was too stressed out to separate from it. I have developed strategies to cope without my rope and my music, and I need to utilize those strategies in order to learn, grow, and experience other things in the real world.

When I think back on my freshman and sophomore years, I feel like I was being sucked into my rope world a lot more than we even realized. My life became a lot more stressful and scary when I entered high school, and the anxiety didn't really alleviate at all until I began my junior year. A lot of the credit can be given to my maturity level, but a lot of it can also be given to the fact I became a lot more understood as high school progressed. It took some time for people to get to know me and for everyone to figure out what worked best for me. The first two years, it was very hard to separate from my mom in the morning because I was walking into an unpredictable environment. I knew I had people at school who were in my corner and who were definitely willing to help me, but it was hard for me to really get that help and things just became a lot more complicated than they had been in middle school. This was probably caused by my hiding skills. I am a professional at masking my autism, except for when I am really anxious and upset. This is why a lot of autistic people tend to fall through the cracks. In middle school, people may have been a little bit fooled at first as a result of that, but that didn't last very long. In high school, it just took a little bit more time to get used to.

For example, there was a time in middle school where I was in my math class. Mrs. Bishop co-taught that class with one of the other math teachers. We were in the middle of taking a test and I was not focused on my test at all. I don't know where my mind was, but it was somewhere far away with absolutely no mathematical equations in sight. There were a lot of quotes hung up on the walls of that classroom, and I used to do my rope to them in my head, so I think that is probably what I was doing. I was twirling my pencil, which was something that would indicate I was stimming (there is usually some type of physical movement involved, even when I am doing my rope in my head). After a few minutes, I looked over and Mrs. Bishop was drinking out of her water bottle and staring right at me. I immediately kind of snapped out of it when I noticed her looking at me because I thought I was going to get in trouble for not being focused on my test. I turned my pencil the right way in my fingers and I tried to make it look like I was working. I turned back to her to see if she was still looking and she was screwing on the lid of her water bottle, but still staring right at me. She ended up telling Mrs. Madrigal, the other math teacher, that my test score couldn't count and I would need to take it again at a different time. She knew I was doing my rope in my head and she had only ever heard about my rope by word of mouth from my mom and I. Somehow, she just got it. When I got to high school, they got it too, but it just took a little bit longer. And when I was starting high school, I was still deep in the trenches of my anxiety and figuring myself out. There were people who really tried to understand me and get me what I needed, but I was really struggling at that time.

At first, I think that people thought my mom was just being overbearing because they couldn't see what was going on inside of me. My mom had been told once that I was her first teenage girl, which implied she just wasn't used to teenage girl dramatics, but I actually do have an older sister and my mom was a teenage girl herself at one time, so she knew this was not just completely teenage drama. My mom has always been a huge advocate for me and she has fought to get me what I need my whole life. There were times where it was definitely uncomfortable for her to go in and have a conversation with somebody about what I needed, but it HAD to be done and she was always willing to do it. There are a lot of struggles that come along with having autism. It is extremely difficult to be on the inside of autism, but it should also be noted that it is hard to be an advocate for an autistic person as well. This is especially true when people don't understand it or accept it. Understanding and acceptance are two of the biggest things that people like me need. If I were to tell you anything about how you could be more accepting of the autism community, I would say that you need to listen to autistic people. There are many voices out there. This is my story, but there are tons more. We all have a lot of things to say, even those of us who are non-verbal. It hurts when people act like autistic people are a burden or talk about autism like it is a tragedy. We can do a lot of the things you can do. We just have a different way of doing them. Talk to us. We have a voice.

Once I got to high school, people didn't come out to meet my mom and I at the car much anymore. My resource teacher, Mr. Texara, did sometimes come out, but I was a little bit more capable of at least getting myself into school at this point. However, on the occasion that my mom did leave me in the car to go inside, it was one of the hardest, yet best moments on those mornings. It was hard because I was still having to face getting into school that day and I was unsure of what was going to happen. It was the best because it gave me a chance to sort out my thoughts. I have learned over the years that when I am in a meltdown state, what I need the most is to be left alone. In the car, there was minimal background noise. It was quiet and I was able to calm myself down. I think that it helps to go somewhere with hardly any stimulation in those moments. I will be able to bring myself back out of a meltdown if I am alone and it is quiet. If someone is trying to talk to me during those times, it can be helpful, but it can also make things a whole lot worse. Now as an adult, I know what to do if I feel this way. Go to my car, take a deep breath, sit in there for a few minutes, and just think. I will certainly cry, but that is okay because I am able to think about what is bothering me and come up with ideas of what to do. It is really helpful for me to be alone with my thoughts. I wish more people had known that when I was younger. Put me in a room with the lights off and little to no noise. I will be able to regulate my emotions eventually.

There was an aide in high school named Lupe who was a great person for me and she was someone I really connected with. She became the person who I went to when I was having a hard time in the mornings or during the school day. They gave me her schedule, so I knew where to find her at any given moment. She put a lot of effort into making sure I was comfortable and she was also a huge comic relief. I had moments where I depended on her because I was in desperate need of someone who understood me and I truly felt like she did. She would also talk to me about my autism and that meant a lot to me because it made me feel like she cared. Mr. Texara had been my health teacher my freshman year and then he had switched over to Special Ed, which made him my resource teacher. When he was just my health teacher, he was still someone who cared to help me in a lot of ways. I had a few meetings my freshman year and he was one of two teachers that always made a point to come to them. He has told me that I was one of his "favorite" students and I don't know why. I gave him a run for his money. Like I said, I really think I was crazy and I gave people a HARD time, but he never gave up on me. He wanted to understand me and he put in that effort to make sure he did. Because of that, I had a lot more success in my junior and senior years of high school.

It took me a long time in high school to go straight to him when I was upset. A lot of times, I went and called my mom on the phone in one of the bathroom stalls. He was always more than willing to help me, but it took me a long time to really warm up to the high school in general. Also, I was getting increasingly sick and tired of people seeing me in one of my anxious and crying messes, and I could ensure nobody would be looking at me if I was in a bathroom stall. There were always people in Mr. Texara's room who would see me, and I just didn't want that to happen anymore. However, if I called my mom, Mr. Texara always got word within a few minutes. Eventually, I did start going to him because I knew he would help me and I truly knew that he was on my side. I remember knowing he was on his prep period and there would not be any kids in his room when I went in there the first time. He almost cried because he was so touched. It was pretty much a breakthrough in my high school career.

Before there were people who were put in place to help me, I sat in the library by myself after I got dropped off. The librarian was a good friend of one of my cousins and she was very kind to let me stay with her like that, but I do wish I would have had someone who made the effort to talk to me and figure out what I needed. I think I was really in need of that and I didn't even realize it at the time. The librarian did talk to me, but it was normal conversation. What I feel like I was missing right at the beginning of high school was someone I could talk to about what I was feeling and what I could do to improve. I didn't know exactly where to go for help and it was all still really fresh and new for me. There was one morning that I had been in the library for a couple of hours, and I probably would have just sat in there all day. I looked up from my phone and I saw my brother Austin walking in the door of the library. He was there to pick me up. I had been talking to my mom on the phone and she had finally just sent him to come get me. I wrote a paper not long after that, and I dramatically described him as, "My knight in shining armor walking through the doors of the library."

Around this time, I occasionally felt like people were walking on eggshells around me. Even though the stereotypes of autism tell you that those on the spectrum struggle with social cues, I am actually a very intuitive person, and I feel like I can pick up on what people are feeling. I struggle with knowing what people mean by the words they use at times, but I can read people fairly well. Therefore, I could somewhat tell when people didn't know what to say to me or they were trying not to upset me. I really hated the feeling that people were walking on eggshells. When you are in a situation where you are seriously incapable of explaining what is wrong with you verbally, it gets very frustrating and overwhelming. You have to show it in other ways and people have to pick up on your signs. There was one morning where I was mad because my mom had just left and I still wasn't completely comfortable. I had my iPod (that I have had for years) in my hands and I threw it down onto the ground (it still works!). The person standing with me, who had been put in charge of helping me that day, looked down at the cement and stared at it for a second. Then, he looked up at me and said, "It's chilly out here today!" I don't think he really knew what to say, but I was trying to show him I was mad and I was still unable to verbally explain why.

One of the most difficult things I have had to learn to overcome is going back into a group of people after I have left upset or anxious. It can be embarrassing, but I have been having to do that my entire life. There were times during my freshman year where nobody knew where I was for forty-five minutes because I would leave class upset and I didn't want to walk back into the classroom. I would usually wait until the bell rang just to avoid walking back in because I was embarrassed. I never left campus, but I would hide out in the bathroom or find a place where people couldn't really see me and I would stay there. There was an afternoon in one of my classes I had brought in a small bottle of soda from my lunch, and I put it on the ground next to my backpack. My teacher had seen the boy sitting next to me eating a sandwich, and so when he came to take it away from him, he saw my soda and he took that away too. I was always guilty by association with the people I sat next to in that class. I liked them a lot, but I don't think the teacher thought as highly of them as I did. There was actually another time in the same class that the teacher brought doughnuts for us to eat, and he didn't give one to anybody in my row because we were talking. I was never one that talked out in class. I hardly even talked when someone was having a direct conversation with me. There was a time my senior year when I was in the middle of a test and my teacher, as a joke, yelled, "Jillian, be quiet!!" Everyone laughed because they knew I never talked. Because of this, I felt it was unfair I didn't get a doughnut (I love doughnuts!), but I was guilty by association.

When the teacher took away my soda, he unscrewed the lid to it and just poured all of it into the trash can while everyone watched. When he was unscrewing the lid, the boy who sat next to me yelled, "That's Jillian's soda!" And then, when my teacher started to pour it out, he yelled, "Oh, you savage!!" While that was funny, it made it a little bit worse because then everyone knew it was my soda. I left class that day and called my mom on the phone. She was in line for her own lunch when I called, so it took her about forty-five minutes to get to me. I waited in the parking lot for her that whole time. Once my mom got there, I went to sit in her car and she went to the office to talk to the principal about what happened.

At the time this happened, I was in a really low spot and it affected me for awhile. When I had gone out and called my mom, I had just been standing against the wall of the school building in the parking lot. It was nearing the end of the school day, and I was worried a bunch of kids were about to come out to their cars. I didn't end up having to see anybody that day when I was super upset, but I did ask my mom on the phone if I could walk across the street to the park. Of course, she told me I couldn't leave campus, and I actually knew I wasn't supposed to do that, but I was just so worried about everyone coming out to the parking lot. When I was in eighth grade, I had seen another student get arrested for running away from campus. I had watched him through the window trying to run away and I saw how that turned out. I think that made me aware of what could happen if I actually left campus and I never tried to do it, but I did threaten it quite a few times. This event with the soda made them more aware of the fact I *could* get lost, but they pretty much knew they would be able to find me somewhere on campus. However, it still made for a few slightly funny mishaps.

When I was a sophomore, I was put into office aiding again, and though I did end up liking it, I kind of went through the same thing I had the first time in seventh grade. I didn't want to do it. It was a different school and I didn't feel as comfortable. The classroom setups were worse in terms of desks being close together, and I was intimidated about having to walk into classrooms full of a bunch of older kids. I definitely voiced to all of the people working with me that I did NOT want to be an office aide. As a result, they decided to make it so I didn't have to take any slips out right at first, and I would only have to help out with the jobs that pertained to staying in the office until I was a little bit more comfortable. However, the secretary didn't know about my autism and she had not been informed of this plan yet. The boy I office aided with had already gone out to take slips and another slip needed to be taken out after he had left, so she handed it to me. I decided it was a better choice to just go take the slip rather than tell her I wasn't going to do that for her. The slip was for Mrs. Piluso, one of the Special Ed. teachers, who I was completely comfortable with. She had gotten to know me a little bit when I was in elementary school, and now she was one of the amazing teachers at the high school. I knew exactly where I was going and I was comfortable and familiar with that room, so I thought it wasn't a big deal. However, that ended up being the one day the particular class I was taking the slip to was nowhere to be found. It turns out they were getting their pictures taken (it was picture day), but before I thought of that, I tried the library, career center, cafeteria, and any other places I could think of. Finally, I decided to try the room where they were taking pictures and I found them there.

While I was searching, about twenty minutes went by, and unbeknownst to me, there was a manhunt happening and *I* was the fugitive! I got a text from one of the aides, Mrs. Gomez, on my phone asking me how my day was going. She was a safe person for me who I had known for many years, so they thought maybe I would tell her I was having a problem and let her know where I was. But since I didn't realize what was happening, all I said was, "Good! How is your day going?" My sister Lindsey called me on the phone because my mom was on her way to the school, even though I didn't know it, and she had asked Lindsey to see if she could get ahold of me. However, I thought talking on the phone was going to be a little bit too much, so I let it go to voicemail and decided I would call her back later. I ran into Lupe in the hallway, who was looking for me, but I didn't know that was what she was doing. I just walked right up to her and started to have a normal conversation. She didn't tell me anything, but we started to walk back to the office together and we went right by one of the janitors. He had one of the staff walkie-talkies clipped to his jeans, and I heard someone's voice come over it and say, "I see her walking with Lupe!" Then, I was really confused. When I walked in the door to the office, a bunch of people turned around and looked at me. Mr. Texara said, "Where have you been?" I said, "I was running a slip." Then, he gave me a high-five. They cancelled my mom before she got there and they all didn't want me to find out that it happened because they were worried it might bother me. However, that didn't last long because I did eventually call Lindsey back and ask her what she wanted.

My junior year, there was another incident similar to this, except I really was missing. Actually, I was hiding in the bathroom. Ever since I realized how much it bothered me to get up in front of people, it had been worked into my plan that I didn't have to. When it was an assignment in a class I was in, I either got an alternative assignment or I got to give a presentation to just the teacher. However, as I got older, it started becoming a problem even more because presentations were getting assigned a lot more frequently. I remember presenting by myself to my English teacher my freshman year and it was literally just my teacher and I in the room, but I couldn't do it. He was really nice about it and asked me questions to answer about my assignment instead, which was actually very helpful. After that, my social learning therapist, Molly, wanted me to get more comfortable speaking in front of people, so I had been having a lot of opportunities to practice. Usually, she and I would prepare it for weeks and then it almost always ended badly. I would get so nervous, my barrier would show up, and then I just would cry and not be able to do it. It happened a lot of times in high school and any little thing could change the outcome.

It goes back to when I talked about how every single aspect of the situation matters. It always will for me. For example, I was doing a debate in my English class my junior year. I had prepared everything I needed to, I was planning on really doing it, and we had it all worked out in such a way to make it as easy for me as possible. Mr. Texara met with me the whole morning of the debate (he even brought me a liter of my favorite soda!) and he called in any adult on campus possible to listen to me give my speech on the State of Jefferson. I did it at least five times one after the other to a lot of teachers and staff members as practice. This definitely was a great idea for the morning of. It gave me a lot of time to work on it and practice it. However, a few groups in my English class had already done their debates the previous day or two, and they had gotten ten minutes to meet with their group at the beginning of class to go over everything before the debate actually started. When I got to class on my day to do the debate, for some reason, we didn't get ten minutes to talk to our group members, and I had been expecting to have that extra time to prepare with them. That threw me off and I subsequently wasn't able to do it. If that hadn't happened, I might have ended up doing it, but anything else could have made it end the same way. It really just does depend on every aspect of the situation and it is best, if you are trying to accomplish something difficult like that, that the environment stays predictable.

When I had my incident my junior year where I was hiding in the bathroom, it was a similar type of situation where one little thing messed me up completely. I was going to be giving a presentation to my history teacher after school was over. Molly was going to come and Mr. Texara was going to be there as well, so I was going to be giving it to a total of three people. That isn't a lot of people and I knew them all perfectly well, but it still made me nervous. I had practiced, but not as much as I should have. I was standing against the wall around the corner from Mr. Texara's classroom, where I was going to be giving the presentation, and I was waiting for Molly. I figured she would walk right by where I was standing and I would meet her before I went in. However, she had gone around the other way that day and she was already in the room, but I didn't know it. My history teacher saw me standing there and he came up to ask if I was ready to go in. It freaked me out because Molly was my person that had been helping me so much with presentations, and I wanted a chance to talk to her before it happened. Because, in reality, I knew I wasn't going to be able to give the presentation that day.

I was experiencing my barrier at that moment, but I couldn't express that to my history teacher. I mean, I never really expressed it to anybody, but he was not somebody who knew me in the way that Molly and Mr. Texara did, even though he was a very nice guy and a wonderful teacher. He wasn't somebody that had dealt with me in those situations and I knew I was on the verge of losing it. That is another thing about these kinds of situations: I never really know how they are going to go. I could feel prepared and ready and then get there and turn into a complete mess. I can predict what will happen, but I never know until I am actually in the situation. I told him I was ready to go in because I knew that was the appropriate response, and I started to follow behind him towards the classroom. He was talking to me as he was walking, but all I was thinking about was, "How do I get out of this situation?" We walked right by the girls bathroom and I decided to make a break for it. I took a few steps backward, opened the door, and slipped in. He kept walking and didn't notice I wasn't behind him anymore until he got to Mr. Texara's room.

I went into one of the stalls, locked the door, and started to have a meltdown. I almost always am in a situation where I am only focused on completely getting out of wherever I am right at that moment, and then once I do, I immediately regret it. The reason for that is because I then have to explain to everybody where I was and why I left. I also knew I needed to apologize to my history teacher for sneaking away from him when he was in the middle of talking to me. I called my mom on the phone and we were in the middle of talking when the door to the bathroom opened. At first, I figured it was just another girl coming in to use the bathroom, so I stayed where I was and didn't think anything of it. But then, I heard a voice yell, "Anybody in here?! Hello?? Anybody in here?!" I didn't know what to do. I knew, by that time, there were probably a lot of people looking for me, so I figured it was someone trying to find me and I chose not to answer. I immediately regretted that though because, as soon as the door started to close, I heard the keys jingle. School had been out for about a half hour and they were starting to lock things up. I ran out of the stall as fast as I could, tears still streaming down my face, but it was too late. I was locked in the bathroom. I tried shaking the handle on the door, I banged on it hoping that someone would hear me, but I was unsuccessful. I then started to freak out even more because now I was locked in the bathroom! That was major anxiety! I think I threw my backpack down, started to pace back and forth, squeezed the palms of my hands, and definitely cried. Those are all things I do when I am having a meltdown. I had shoved my phone in my pocket with my mom still on the other line and I picked it back up. My voice was shaking as I said, "I'm locked in the bathroom!" She told me to hang up and call Molly while she called Mr. Texara. I told Molly what bathroom I was in and she ran up to the janitor, who had just locked me in there, and said, "There is a student in that bathroom!" The janitor let me out a few seconds later and said, "I asked if there was anybody in here! Do you know how to talk?" After about thirty minutes, Molly and I had a good laugh about it, and it has been a source of comedy for all of us ever since. However, in the moment, it was just a little bit terrifying.

I did end up sending an apology email to my history teacher that night and he was very understanding about it. That has always been something I have had to do that seems repetitive and a little bit upsetting. I do think that every time I have sent an apology email to a teacher, it has been needed. Either I left the classroom without permission or I didn't end up doing the debate like I was supposed to, etc. There have been many reasons that apology emails have been sent, and I always have to explain a little bit about my autism when I do it. I have to say things like, "I am so sorry I left the classroom. I was feeling very anxious at that moment and I didn't feel like I could be in there. I hope you understand." I have had a horrible time in college. It is a very new experience, a new place, and a lot of new teachers. At least when I was in high school, I kind of knew what to expect with the teachers because all of my siblings had already gone all the way through. I am the first of my siblings to go to the particular college I attend, and I don't know anything about a teacher when I walk in the room on the first day. Everytime there have been icebreakers, I have had to leave and thus had to send an apology email later. Icebreakers make me way too nervous and my mind will just go a million miles a minute until I finally get out of there.

I have been dropped from a class twice on the first day because I left, and I had to really explain myself after that. There was also one class where I explained myself, went back the next time, and had the same thing happen all over again. I had to finally ask, "Is this a class where these kinds of things are going to happen every single time?" Then, I had to make the decision for myself to find another class and get out of that one. It just wasn't going to work for me. That is my reality. I have to work myself around other people and people aren't always going to understand why things bother me the way they do. It feels counterproductive to be having to apologize for my autism all the time, but that is what it takes to get people to understand. I feel the need to say something along the lines of, "This is how I am. This is what sometimes happens to me, but I am willing to work with you." If I am asking for an alternative assignment, I make sure that I offer plenty of other options, so that they know I am not just trying to get out of something. My psychology teacher my very first semester of college also had autism, but I still had to send that email. Almost all of my teachers have always been receptive and understanding. They just need to be told. That's why advocacy is so important. First, from others. Then, if you are capable, for yourself, but it is a very hard thing to do, and I still struggle with it a lot. In high school, I had my mom to talk for me when I was unable to speak for myself and that was very crucial for me. And, because I was constantly being pushed out of my comfort zone, I am now able to advocate for myself in college. It is hard to send those emails every few months, but it is something I have to do.

Chapter Thirteen: Unplug The Microwave

Things change and we will learn how to cope in our own ways. What is an issue now will not be an issue forever.

I was on anxiety medication for two and a half years of high school. I got it prescribed to me in the middle of my eighth grade year and I took it until the middle of my junior year. It was a blood pressure medication. It was supposed to help me get more sleep, have less anxiety, and it also lowered my blood pressure, which was very high for someone my age. At this point, I honestly don't know if it was helpful to me or not. The three years that I was on it were my worst three years in terms of my anxiety. Ever since my junior year of high school, I have not experienced any form of the chronic anxiety like I had in my earlier years. The only way I can ever imagine myself going back to that state of mind would be if I were in a really tough job situation or something of that sort. I think I would have to be forced to repeatedly go somewhere or do something that was extremely upsetting and anxiety-provoking for me to ever get back to that place of chronic anxiety. Therefore, I don't know if medication is something I will ever need again. I am able to get through my day-to-day life okay and I have found ways to cope with the daily struggles I have. There are always obstacles along the way, but I am able to handle things a lot better now. I am very hopeful that I will never be in one of those really bad spots again.

In the middle of my sophomore year, I had somebody with whom I was very good friends and things were kind of starting to fall apart. It was one of my very bad years. I was still having a lot of trouble, and I was not myself at all. I think the same could be said for my friend. We were both going through a hard time in our lives and neither of us were the type to talk about it to anybody. I hardly ever mentioned my autism to any of my peers, let alone told them about how much I was struggling with it. It just wasn't something I talked about unless I had to, so if one of my friends never saw me during one of my meltdowns on a bad morning, they would have never known I was having a difficult time. There have been two times I can recall where I have been telling someone about the hard times I had in school, and they have said something along the lines of, "No, but I have actual anxiety." This makes it seem like a little bit of a lost cause to even try to explain it to people. However, I also think people have a hard time imagining me in the state that I was in because it did somewhat make me a different person. It affected all parts of my life. Just recently, someone was telling me about how he had a desk in the principal's office when he was younger. I thought he was embarrassed so I said, "I did too." He replied, "I find that very hard to believe." My grandma told me not that long ago that, whenever my mom talked about one of my meltdowns, it surprised her. She lived right next door to me and she never saw me like that. I was such a quiet, well-behaved child that it was almost baffling to hear that I was even having meltdowns let alone the occasional extreme meltdowns I had during those three years. This is where masking can affect autistic people, even with those they are closest to.

There was one time in high school that I was watching the children I worked with as they were playing on the play structure, and one of them came up to tell me that a little girl had said a very bad word. I looked over to where he was pointing and saw this little, petite girl with a big pink bow in her hair skipping with a big smile on her face. I said, "Her?! That girl said that?!" That was how I was. I saved my rage for my parents and my siblings. Even on our big family vacations, my cousins probably wouldn't tell you I was on edge at all, but vacations are actually when I am the *most* on edge. It is a break in my routine. I am in a different place than I am used to, and my opportunities for doing my rope and my music are slim. Any little thing could send me tumbling over the edge and I'll just keep on going. My mom will usually notice if I am getting anxious because of how present I seem in conversations, how restless I am, or how irritable I get. Then, she will give me the time I need to decompress. But, as best as I possibly could, I showed those signs to my mom and nobody else. Occasionally, it becomes too much and I will get outwardly upset, but I have always tried my very hardest not to ever let anybody else see that side of me. Because of this, it makes complete sense that I never confided in my friends at school about what I was going through, and I think this started to become a problem for me with this particular friendship.

I think it was happening a little bit on both ends, but the fact I felt more anxious and misunderstood than I ever had made me almost unable to put up with anything else. My friend and I kind of just stopped communicating with each other in all forms and that was the end of that. It has never been repaired, but at first, I really did not like that. I thought about it for a long time, I wrote out practice messages on a notepad, reread it, edited it, and finally sent it to her. It was a very long message where I explained what I had been dealing with, and I expressed to her I would have never wanted to hurt somebody I care about. I still care about her, and I don't like having that kind of turmoil with anybody, but when I sent that message, I had the mindset I was going to accept whatever she gave me in return. I was hoping for a positive response, but I willed myself to be okay if that wasn't what I ended up getting. In the end, I didn't get a response; however, I surmised I had attempted to fix it and that was all I could do. Now, it was off of my shoulders and it gave me a sense of closure. That is how I have always been with any kind of negative experiences I have had with other people. If I can do anything, I want to try to repair it, and if that doesn't work, I just like to have the mindset that it isn't on my shoulders anymore. I absolutely hate having negative interactions with people, and I want to fix it as much as I possibly can.

On the contrary, I once expressed to one of my other classmates that I didn't like her, and it was like walking into something I hate. If someone had told me they didn't like me, I would have been so upset and mad. I didn't want her to feel that way towards me, and though she didn't ever seem to care, it still made me feel rotten inside. This happened to me a lot more when I was going through my hard times in school. I let people know when they made me mad. I didn't hold my tongue. I even asked Mr. Texara to leave me alone once. He did, but then I felt horrible. My mom said I actually asked him to do that twice, but I don't even remember doing it the second time. Often times, my memory was a little bit cloudy after one of my bad mornings. I wasn't always receptive or understanding to things people said to me. Because I was so on edge, I got irritated and offended fast. There was one time when I was an office aide that I got super annoyed at all of the teachers because they used to keep the microwave in the teacher's room plugged in. There was a sign on the front of the microwave that read, "Please unplug the microwave after you use it." But everyday, I had to unplug the microwave because it was always left plugged in. One day, I was just like, "I'm done!" and I wrote out an angry note to put on the microwave, but then I thought better of it. After all, those were all of the teachers who had authority over me that I was dealing with, so I don't think that would have been a good idea. I just got angry very easily because of the situation I was in. I was just done with having to deal with all of this and it was affecting me in other situations that had nothing to do with it.

There was one afternoon where I had seen my mom's car on campus, but I hadn't previously known she was there. I knew it was her car because I had the license plate number memorized. I used to do this a lot when I was younger. I mainly paid attention to the three letters in the middle. I didn't put as much emphasis on the numbers, unless it was a truck and it only had one letter. If I see a familiar car in town, I always look at the license plate and that is how I know if it is the person I suspect it is or not (if I know them well enough to have memorized their license plate number). A lot of times, I even pay more attention to the license plate number than I do the actual car. When I recognized the license plate on my mom's car, I figured she was on campus somewhere, and then I immediately wanted to get to her. I had already asked my Child Development teacher, Mrs. Miller, if I could go to Mr. Texara's room and she had told me I could. If I was ever feeling extra anxious or having a really hard time, I was allowed to go to his room for a little bit of a break. When she was writing me my pass, I don't know what made me say it, but I said, "I'm having a really hard time." Mrs. Miller is a super nice lady, and she was always willing to help me. I think I just felt comfortable enough to confide in her like that, but also, thinking back on it, it seems like a little bit of a cry for help. She got a sad look on her face and said, "I'm so sorry." After I left her classroom was when I noticed the car.

I found my mom and I think the reason I wanted to go to her was because she was the safest person I had. I still didn't feel that comfortable at school, and when I saw the car there, I wanted to have that comfort I knew she would give me. However, it didn't end up being a good thing because she was obviously having a meeting about me, and I just burst through the door like I owned the place. Then, once I was in there and they were talking about things that were hard for me to hear and think about, I freaked out and had a huge meltdown. It is a horrible day for me to think back on. That was one of the times where I really just felt like, "What am I doing? Why am I acting like this? Who have I become?" It was like I was a different person watching myself do the things I was doing. There was not even anything happening that day that warranted a meltdown like that, but it was just me being so pushed to my breaking point because of this intense anxiety I was constantly experiencing. That was one of the main times where I feel like I was crazy. I know I wasn't crazy, but I was losing my mind. I didn't want to be thought of that way, but I felt that way and I'm sure I looked that way. I was trapped. I couldn't stop my own head from being so anxious, guarded, and pessimistic. I was two different people. On one hand, I didn't want to be having these struggles and was trying so hard to be normal and keep it all together. On the other hand, I was also one that was incapable of keeping it together, who was letting the anxiety take over my life, and who didn't seem to be making any positive strides. I was going backwards. I felt like I needed my mom for everything, and I was being forced to do things I didn't want to do. I was being forced to do things that were incredibly hard for me, and I was having to do them every single day. That day was horrible and those years were dark. I just was not happy at all and I was really, really struggling.

After I had been on my medication for a few months, I was unhappy with the results I was getting because my anxiety was still a huge problem. It was still interfering with every part of my life. As a result of that, I wanted to take more of my medication because I was thinking that if I took more, it would alleviate my anxiety more. When I first started taking it, I had the mindset that it would be like magic. It would take away my anxiety and all would be well in the world. I would never have to deal with these issues again. And, at first, I did kind of feel that way, but I think it was my mind tricking me into feeling that way. After awhile when it wasn't working the way I wanted it to, I asked if I could increase my dosage. It was a very tiny pill and my prescribed dosage was a quarter of a tablet a day. I took it smashed up in yogurt every night. For some reason, I was completely incapable of swallowing it whole, even though it was miniscule. My grandma finally taught me how to, but leading up to that point, I needed it to be put in yogurt in order to take it.

Right around the time I was starting to feel disappointed in it, we were having a family party for Easter and I was so anxious that I could not go. My mom stayed home with me while I cried and the rest of my family went ahead without us. At that point, I was just frustrated because I had thought I was getting something that was going to take away this problem for me, and it was not doing that. Maybe it was taking some of the edge off, but I don't know when I felt that other than right at the beginning. I felt horrible about myself. Not in terms of appearance, but in terms of just who I was as a person. I had a very hard time with family parties because of the volume of people and the expected social interactions. I still usually find time to excuse myself to the bathroom for a few minutes while at a family party, even though I do tremendously better now than I ever did. The hard part about it for me is the fact that I love having intimate conversations. They make me feel good about myself because I am getting to know someone and share my thoughts with them. It is one of my favorite things to do, but it can be so difficult at the same time. I eventually made it to the party that day, but it wasn't without a lot of barriers, anxiety, and sadness.

When I was in elementary school, I had been on a different kind of medication. It was an antidepressant medication and it was in liquid form. I drank a cup of it every day. It was supposed to also help with the OCD component of my autism, but it actually had the opposite effect on me. It wound me up completely and I kept giving into a bunch of weird impulses. I was having such vivid dreams at night that it didn't feel like I had slept a wink by the time I woke up. I also became obsessed with tapping people on the shoulder. There was a night where Austin had just had a basketball game and he was upset about the outcome. I wasn't helping his frustration. I was just fixated on his shoulder and tapping it over and over again. He exclaimed, "This medicine is making her worse!" I only stayed on that medication for a few weeks because it seemed to be doing more harm than good. I don't remember not feeling like I slept, I don't remember ever tapping anyone on the shoulder, and I only remember drinking the first cup I ever drank. For some reason, I just blacked out when I was on that medication. When I got on my anxiety medication in eighth grade, I truly did feel like I had immediate relief. I almost thought I was experiencing the placebo effect because it just seemed to be working so great right at first. However, it still was not what I had envisioned it to be and, after a while, that feeling wore off. It wasn't helping as much as I wanted it to help, and since I had felt so great about it right at first, it was like a let down. I wanted my anxiety to just go away.

In October of my freshman year, my doctor finally did grant me an increase in my dosage. I was now allowed to take half of the pill every day rather than just a quarter. It was something I had really wanted and I was really looking forward to it because, though I was wrong, I had the idea it would rid me of all my anxiety. That was the goal of a lifetime for me. There were some days where I took my medication at night and some days that I took it in the morning before school. The first day I took half instead of a quarter, I took it in the morning right before I went to school. I had a good morning that day, meaning I went to school perfectly fine. My mom had curled my hair and everything. That always indicated I was having a good day because it meant I felt good about myself! In middle school, the same could be said about makeup. I caked it on and I wore everything under the sun. Lipstick, mascara, foundation, eyeshadow, etc. It is embarrassing now, but at the time, I really loved it, and it meant I was having a good day at school. When Mr. Pfaff saw me in the morning, he would know it was going to be a good day if I had my hair and makeup done. Once I got to high school, I abandoned makeup completely. I was just too focused on trying to survive. I didn't really start wearing it again until my senior year, and after that October morning my freshman year, I never curled my hair again in high school either.

My first class of the day was my biology class. I walked up the stairs to the science building and I found my seat. We had a lab we were working on, so after a few minutes, I met up with my lab group at one of the tables. We were working with chemicals, which meant there were a lot of fumes and smells circulating in the air, and about forty minutes after I got there, I started to feel really sick. I got this horribly uncomfortable feeling right in the pit of my stomach, and I sat down to see if it would go away a little bit. After a few seconds, I stood back up and then I knew it: I was going to throw up. I have only thrown up twice in my life that I can remember. Once when I was very little and once when I was fourteen. The second time at fourteen, I yelled, "HELP!!!" to my mostly sleeping household in the middle of the night because I seriously didn't know what throwing up was like. I am not accustomed to that feeling so I just did what I thought was best in my biology class that day. I started walking towards the trash can, but I got so lightheaded that I stopped. I couldn't see the person standing right in front of me and, a few seconds later, instead of throwing up in the trash can, I hit my head on it on the way down. When I came to, it was like a scene from a movie. My teacher and my lab group hovering over me going, "Are you okay? Did you collapse?" I panicked and my "throwing up drama" came back full force as I kept saying, "I don't know! I was dizzy!" I got to leave school very soon after that and headed straight for the doctor. She thought it was a mixture of everything, but that was the first and last time I ever took my medication with the increased dosage. At least my hair looked good, though.

At the beginning of my junior year, I got really sick and I didn't take my medicine for about a week because I was taking so many other things in order to get better. After that, we realized I was able to function without it quite well. My junior year is where my life got a lot better in many ways, which made my anxiety lessen a little bit on its own, and the medication was no longer something I needed to keep me afloat. Of course, I still had the situational anxiety, but the chronic (horrific) anxiety was pretty much gone once I got about a month into my junior year. Even though I struggled with being on a medication, and it did a number on my mental health both times, there are people who have had incredible success with it. One experience should not dictate what another person does to cope or help with their own situation. We are all just doing our best and my hope is that everyone finds something to help them deal with their struggles and get through the tough times. Miss Proctor had told me that when I was first getting on my medication in eighth grade. She said, "It probably won't be something you will always need, but it is something that could be helpful to you right now." At the time, I didn't realize that, because I couldn't foresee a life without anxiety. It was so present in everything I did, and I had gotten so used to it being there, that I couldn't fathom it would ever go away. But my day did come. While I still live with an intense form of social, situational, and not-able-to-shut-my-mind-off types of anxiety, I am no longer crippled by it. It was almost debilitating from my third grade year to the middle of high school, and while a lot of those times are difficult for me to think back on, I can almost say now it was worth it. I learned a lot from all of those horrible moments, events, days, weeks, and years. My mom told me once that an autism interventionist said to her, "Crying is learning." I think it is true, even though I hate it at the same time. Those years taught me an incredible amount about myself and who I am as a person.

The media teaches a lot of things about autism and a lot of those things don't necessarily fit with what is true. There are many stereotypes surrounding autism, and if you see an autistic person portrayed in a movie or on a show, they are generally painted as the "autistic savant" type. I also feel like they occasionally are depicted as a somewhat emotionless person. They typically show them as having extreme difficulties with social interaction and eye contact. I am here to say that all of those things may exist in people on the spectrum. There are autistic people who are geniuses and struggle a lot socially. However, the spectrum is huge. You cannot categorize autistic people by saying they are either on one end of the spectrum or the other. There are people on every inch of the spectrum. I feel like part of the reason people sometimes don't want to acknowledge autism in a person, or they think autism is a reason to express to someone that they are so sorry they have to deal with this, is because people do not have an accurate understanding of all the different ways that autism can look.

Most autistic people I know feel things very deeply and are extremely empathetic towards humans, animals, and even sometimes objects. I can't throw anything away because I'm really certain that my candy wrapper has feelings. That doesn't fit the stereotypes. It is frustrating to me that autism has such a stigma surrounding it because I know all of the wonderful qualities that many autistic people have. Autism makes up how a person is and that is why I think it should be accepted. I understand people who don't want to see someone they love struggle and I know that autism is really hard in many ways. If it wasn't, I wouldn't have written this book. However, when you have autism, you get to see the world in such a different way. To me, it is neat how the reward when you're autistic is so much bigger because of how much harder you have to work for things. Tiny little obstacles in other people's lives can be huge mountains to climb for us. It is a huge accomplishment to overcome them and it is worthy of celebrating every single time. Autistic children will grow up to be strong, resilient, hardworking, and incredible autistic adults with a story to tell. You can choose to see autism as a myriad of problems and there are times where I wish with everything in me that I wasn't autistic. But autism is who I am and I don't want to change who I am. There is always hope for the things you wish to accomplish. It doesn't matter what walk of life you have experienced. There is always hope to overcome the obstacles that life throws your way and reach the goals you have for yourself. Do what you think is best. Congratulate yourself along the way because, I'm telling you, there will be so many times where, as family members and individuals with autism, you deserve to be congratulated.

I grew up in a very religious household and my parents took us to church every single Sunday for many years. When I was little, my mom was the youth group leader and we were very involved in our church. I was a member of the children's choir at the church my grandparents attend right across the street from ours. I have spent lots of time at both of these churches throughout my life. I have always had that background and that foundation, but when I was having all of my struggles my eighth, ninth, and tenth grade years, I was not receptive to any of it. I was very bitter, mad at the world, and just so frustrated with my situation. I outwardly expressed to my parents and siblings that I was NOT a believer and I attribute this to two things. One being, like I said before, I was so mad, frustrated, and bitter, but the other being that it didn't make sense to me. I am a very literal thinker and I always have been. It makes for many jokes amongst my family members.

When I was in fourth grade, my brother-in-law, Teddy, chose me to interview for an assignment he had in his psychology class. It had something to do with the understanding of the English language at different ages, and I was his youngest subject. He asked me, "What does the term 'The apple doesn't fall far from the tree' mean?" I thought about it for a few seconds and then I answered, "It means it landed on a branch." When I was meeting my kindergarten teacher for the first time a few days before school started, she asked me if I liked punch and cookies. I was shocked that she asked me this and I said, "Why would I punch a cookie? I like to eat them." While it makes for a lot of jokes and laughter among my family members, this trait I have made it easy for me to not be able to make sense of a lot of the things I heard about in church. When I got to the point where I had no hope for myself or my situation, I never thought it would get better. That was just how my life was always going to be. There was nothing I could do. But I was lacking so much. I didn't have faith in anything. I just figured I was plagued with all of these issues, anxieties, and barriers and that was the story of my life. What was the point? My mom was very understanding of me feeling the way that I felt towards all of it because she knew why I thought the way I did. She knew that it might not make a whole lot of sense to someone like me, and she tried to work with me on understanding it.

At the very end of my sophomore year, my mom and I were shopping at the dollar store, and I came across a book that seemed really interesting to me. It was about a married couple that had been in a small airplane crash and had received major, life-threatening injuries. It was written by the wife who had to spend months in the hospital, and three in a coma, while her four young children were cared for by her sisters and her husband who was recovering himself. She still, twelve years later, deals with injuries that are a result of their accident. She had grown up in a church that is vastly different from the one I grew up in, and she was raising her children the same way. She was very devoted and faithful and, even when she was on the verge of death and suffered those horrible injuries, her faith never wavered once. She was steadfast in her beliefs and her convictions, and she credits a lot of her recovery to that. I have read that book probably twenty times since then because I have always found it so amazing she was able to do that. I wasn't able to do it and my situation seems like it was way less difficult than hers was.

But after I read her book, I finally realized I could be standing in the way of my own success. Of course, I still have my autism and I always will, but when I finally gave my life up to God, I experienced a sense of peace I hadn't ever experienced before. People that knew me before my sophomore year and that know me now would probably say I am a much happier person because I truly am. Now, I know there is a plan for me. There is a reason I am living this life, and there is a reason I have autism. I think I am called to share it in this way. I know not everyone has the same beliefs I do, and it doesn't have a whole lot to do with my autism in general, but it is a part of my life, and it is something that really helped me. It gave me the ability to still deal with my inevitable struggles, but deal with them with a sense of peace, courage, love, and faith.

After I read that book a couple of times, I reached out to the woman who wrote it, and she told me I touched her deeply. I follow her life online and she is someone that makes me feel less alone. One of the biggest problems I experienced as a teenager is the feeling that I just didn't fit in with other teenagers. A lot of that could be because of my autism. I'm just not really like other kids my age in many ways. Molly has encouraged me a lot in the last few years to do more things with kids my own age, and that is something that I want to do. I understand her reasoning for encouraging me to do so, but I feel conflicted about it. I feel like I relate more to adults than I do to people my own age, and I also relate to children more than I do to people my own age. My mom tells me that I have an old soul and I do. I think I relate more to adults because my thinking is more like an adult. I kind of skipped over the bad-teenage-decision phase. I was the annoying kid who told all of the other kids, "That sounds like a terrible idea." I followed all of the rules because I never wanted to do anything that could potentially get me into a bad situation. I relate more to children because I still possess a lot of the innocence that children possess. I love working with kids because they accept you no matter what you bring to the table. I think we should all be more like them in a lot of ways. I look at a lot of people my own age, and I just don't have much of an interest in a lot of the things they find fun. I am scared of a lot of it as well. I am on a few autism support groups on Facebook and I was surprised to find out that I am not nearly the only one who feels this way.

Throughout school, I had a few really good friends and a lot of acquaintances, but I have always had one really great friend who has been with me forever. Her name is Allison and she has a lot of the same core beliefs that I do. We have been friends since first grade when we were in the same class together, which has been almost sixteen years now. We just kind of get each other, we think the same things are funny, and we like all of the same stuff. We like to do things like go to the park, drive around, eat fast food, reminisce on our childhood by listening to High School Musical, and work on projects, such as vision boards at the beginning of every year. We have a Christmas tradition of getting a hot chocolate and driving around to look at lights. Those are the simple things I find fun to do with people and I am so thankful I have such a great companion to do them with. We bond with each other in really simple ways and that is what I love about our friendship.

I love driving in the car with people because I feel like it almost forces intimate conversations I don't always know how to have. To me, a car is the best setting for those. I drive my family nuts because I will ask them almost every single night, "Anyone want to drive to the gas station just for kicks?!" They never want to, so then I will say something like, "But it is so boring here! I've been home all day!" or I'll find something worthy of celebrating, such as, "But we need to celebrate the fact that I made a phone call two weeks ago! It was really stressful for me!" Then, we all end up piled into the car together on the way to the gas station for no reason at all and, believe it or not, I am almost always the only one that has fun! Mainly, my dad will end up taking me somewhere or, even if I didn't ask, I love to go on trips to town with him. It is kind of our thing because we play loud music, and he tells me to take my feet off the dash. Every time! Whenever he goes to town for anything, I love to tag along with him, but I don't know if he really enjoys it like I do. However, I think we should all live by my saying, "In the world of autism, every small step is a huge success," and celebrate all of the little accomplishments along the way! Celebrate it however you like to celebrate things (a drive to town sounds like fun), and know that you are amazing and admirable! You will find ways to cope and everything will be okay eventually.

Chapter Fourteen: Special Problems

Come into our world. Even if it seems as though our door is shut, it isn't. We have a lot more to offer than you realize.

    I am definitely not someone who has a lot of friends, and I have had a harder time with this as I have gotten older. In high school, I had many people I talked to in my classes who I loved to be around, and I would definitely consider some of them to be friends to me. However, I have a hard time maintaining friendships, keeping friends, and just getting close enough to a person for them to consider me a friend. I have found I do a lot better when people ask me questions or try to talk to me. I know this is not a great way to be because it isn't always going to work out in my favor. I am not always going to be able to count on people reaching out to me first or trying to initiate a conversation with me. If I just wait around for that all the time, I might not ever have anybody trying to talk to me. (I think I just figured out my problem!) In order to have a friendship, I have to understand it is a two-way street, and I need to put in that effort also. However, it is hard for me because I get so nervous, I tense up, and I usually do not know what to say. Most conversations I have are started by the other person. When someone does make that effort with me, it always makes me feel elated. I am usually honored that people try to talk to me, and when I feel like I did a good job responding and I wasn't thrown off guard, I just feel really happy for the opportunity. Like I said, conversations are actually one of my favorite things, and that is because they have the ability to bring me this feeling. However, I also feel like I mess up a lot, and then it has the ability to have the opposite effect on me as well. But, mainly, it is a very helpful thing for me when someone gives me that initial push in a conversation. Just like the hardest part of a bad morning was sometimes just walking through the door to a classroom, the hardest part of a conversation for me is simply starting it.

There have been two times since I got out of school where my old classmates have come up to me. One time, I was at a birthday party for a close family friend, and the other time, I was at a pizza place waiting for my order to be ready to take home. At the pizza place, a boy I went to school with asked me how I was doing, and at the birthday party, it was a girl classmate who came up and asked me if I was liking college. I was taken aback both times because neither of them were people I had ever really talked to while we were in high school. When we were in elementary school, we had been in some of the same classes, so they were people I had known since I was little, but when we got older, we just never talked to each other. When I was at the pizza place, I had seen him, but I didn't have any intention of initiating a conversation with him. I was just sitting there looking through my phone and waiting for my name to be called. At the birthday party, I was sitting at a table with my dad eating nachos. I had also noticed her that time, but I didn't plan on initiating a conversation with her either. Both times this happened, I felt really good about the fact they cared enough to stop and talk to me. Both of those conversations highlight that fact about me though. I won't start a conversation. It makes me so nervous. However, when someone else tries to have one with me, it makes me feel so important, and without realizing it, they were both helping me improve in that area. Anyone who initiates a conversation with me is doing that.

I have always had problems with communication. A lot of times, the barrier I experience is also very present in my ability to communicate, and it gets a lot worse if I am in an anxiety/meltdown state. I will shut down and it is almost like all forms of my communication go out the window. Once I am in that state, words basically have to be pried out of me. My mom used to tell me, "I can't help you if I don't know what's wrong." The reason she would say that is because I would be noticeably upset, but I wouldn't be talking. I just won't say anything. It is almost like everything about the situation is too overwhelming that I can't bring myself to speak. It is weird for me because when I am in that situation, I just can't put into words what I am feeling. I don't know why this is, but it is extremely difficult. I have said before that sometimes I didn't even know what I was feeling, and that made it nearly impossible to be able to explain to anybody else what I was feeling. A lot of times, I would get even more upset when I knew people didn't understand, even though I completely get why they didn't understand. It was just frustrating to feel so misunderstood and unable to communicate my needs to the people who were trying to help me. It was scary for me because I knew they were the source of my help. What my mom would say was completely true. They couldn't help me if they didn't know what was wrong, and I so badly needed the help but, for whatever reason, I didn't feel like I could express it. There were some moments where I wasn't successfully able to express it, even though I tried to. My resource teachers used to implement asking me questions while I was in my shutdown mode as a way to figure out what was wrong. For example, they would ask me things like, "Did someone hurt your feelings? Are you nervous about something?" I would usually shake my head until they asked me the right question and then they would know where to go from there. Eventually, they would figure out what to do. Verbally, I couldn't say it, which made this technique they used really great for all of us in terms of being able to solve the problem.

There was a time in eighth grade where I had a presentation assignment in my English class. My English teacher, Mrs. McNally, was so accommodating to me, and she was one of the best teachers I have ever had, but presentations were incredibly terrifying for me. I was in a group for this particular assignment, and it was worked out among my group members and my teachers that I would write the information we gathered onto the slides of the powerpoint presentation. However, *they* would stand up in front of the classroom and actually give the presentation. I didn't have to stand up there with them as long as I did the writing portion of the assignment. Back then, I would even have a ton of anxiety if my group members were giving a presentation I had worked on. Even if I knew that I didn't have to get up and talk, just having my classmates look at something I had put together was enough to give me a whole bunch of anxiety for a few mornings. Because of this, Mr. Pfaff and Miss Proctor had decided I needed to be in the room. There were times I was granted the opportunity to leave the room for that period of time, but they figured the first step at getting me more comfortable was being able to stay in there for the presentation, so that was the plan for that day. However, I kept having an enormous amount of anxiety toward this presentation and having to stay in the classroom.

I spent some mornings in Mr. Pfaff's office with him when I had exceptionally bad days, and the day of my English presentation was one of those days. Most times, they were able to get me to class eventually, but sometimes it was just too much. Whenever that happened, I put together his grand schedule for him. He had a big white board in his office, and it had little magnets with the names of all of the teachers and the school subjects on them. The teachers' names were color coordinated based on the subjects they taught, and I would place the teachers' names on the left hand side of the board and then put a magnet for each subject next to their name. Eventually, it stretched all the way out with seven total magnets (the seven class periods each teacher had). I was fascinated with this board. I had all of the teachers' schedules memorized just from paying attention to everything I saw and heard about the classes other kids were in. I was able to piece it all together, and he would stick me next to that board on really bad days to get me to calm down. In a way, it was kind of like another form of doing my rope and it did indeed calm me down. On the morning of the English presentation, I was putting it back together as I talked to my mom on the phone. She was telling me, "Sometimes, you have to do things that you don't want to do." She was referring to the fact I had to stay in the classroom for the presentation my group was giving. I got my signature eighth grade attitude and said, "Well, just what if I don't want to do what I don't want to do?!" It was causing me a lot of anxiety knowing I was going to have to be in the room while the presentation happened, even though I knew I didn't have to present it myself. They all knew that, but there was a little bit more to it this time than I was able to get across to them. My anxiety was getting increasingly worse because I knew they weren't understanding what was wrong.

The actual work I had done on the presentation was what was bothering me. I thought I had written too much and it was going to be too long. I felt like this because of the other presentations I had seen the other groups give the day before. I didn't ever directly come out and say that, which made them all just assume it was just my usual presentation anxiety. They didn't realize I actually wanted to change my work. I just could not express that to them. I had spent the morning trying to convince them all not to let my group members present it to the class, but they didn't understand the whole problem. They just assured me that it was fine. When I got to class at the very end of the day (it was a very long day!), I was really worried. I wished I had gotten some time to turn my paragraphs into bullet points to shorten the powerpoint because that is what I had seen some of the other groups do. However, I wasn't able to do that because I hadn't voiced what the real issue was.

The first slide came up onto the screen and one of the kids in my class said, "That is way too long." It was the comment I had walked into school afraid of that morning. I asked my teacher if I could go to Miss Proctor's room and she granted me permission to do so. Once I got there, I didn't start crying right away. I just sat down in one of the chairs I always sat in. Two of the kids in my English class came to get me. It was always very kind when the kids cared enough to come check on me when they knew I had left upset. However, I also didn't ever want my peers to see me like that so it sometimes made it harder for me. One of them asked Miss Proctor if I was ready to go back, and she said, "Jill knows what she needs to do." At that moment, I still hadn't told her what had happened so she thought I had just failed at staying in the room while the presentation was happening. Right after she said that, I started to fall apart and she sent the kids back to class. She took me out into the hallway and I finally told her I had been worried that the presentation was too long and somebody had said that it *was* too long. Mr. Pfaff turned the corner when I was really upset. He was on his way to take care of something and he had come across us there. Normally, I only cried in the mornings and he said, "What happened?" She told him, "Somebody said that her presentation was too long. She said she was trying to tell us that." At that moment, I could tell they both felt bad. They are people that know about the communication barrier, but sometimes it is just that: a communication barrier. There are times where it doesn't even get through to the ones who understand it the best.

Being in a group presentation has always been extremely hard for me and it hasn't gotten easier for me yet. Especially now in college, it is extremely difficult for me because I have to explain to my classmates why I won't be presenting with them, and I am always nervous that they might not take it well. After all, it makes it harder for them because they have to pick up the slack for me. I had a situation in eighth grade that has impacted my anxiety about this because my group members *did* get mad at me. I was in a group with two other kids and it had all been worked out that I wasn't going to get up in front of the class. When it came time for them to do the presentation, my teacher kept trying to get me to stand up in front of the class with my group. I think it was just a misunderstanding of what was happening. He didn't completely realize I didn't have to stand up there at all, and I don't think he knew he was upsetting me by trying to get me to do so, especially after it had been previously worked out that I didn't have to. I went in there feeling safe knowing I didn't have to stand up there, which made it upsetting that now I was being asked to. I just told him I wasn't going to do it.

After they were done, one of the people in my group completely ripped into me about it. She was just going off and questioning me about why I didn't feel like I had to get up there with them. Once she started, my other group member just kind of joined in with her, and started doing the same thing. My autism was still a secret, and I didn't know how to answer her questions without giving myself away. However, she wasn't letting up, so I finally just gave in and said, "I have special problems." That was my way of saying it without actually saying it and it was the best explanation that I knew how to give her. She gave me a really dirty look like I was being completely ridiculous and she said, "Well, in the real world and in college, nobody is going to care about your special problems." I haven't run into any problems with teachers not accommodating me in college thus far, so I consider her wrong about that at this point. However, what she said was something that other adults have said to me at different times about the same subject, but in a much nicer way. I needed to be prepared for the change in how my accommodations would look when I got to college. But it was a lot harder for me to hear it from one of my peers because it wasn't coming from a place of concern. This incident still affects me when I have to explain myself to my group members. However, that has been the only time so far that anyone has reacted negatively to it. Most of the time, my group members are very understanding.

When I was in high school, my communication barrier got worse. I had a more ongoing form of the communication barrier, and I was unable to get through to people. In particular, there was a situation where I was frustrated because I didn't feel like I was doing well in my math class. I have always had a lot more trouble with math than I do with any other subject. I enjoyed English and history classes. Once I got to high school, I didn't have to take P.E. classes anymore. I went for the first week, and it was just too much, especially with all of the additional things I was dealing with. If anything, I am very grateful I was exempt from that portion of it. Rather than take it as a class during the school day like everyone else, I did P.E. at home and my brother Austin was my "teacher." I get a lot of physical exercise just by doing the things that are a part of my normal routine, such as my rope and running in the driveway with my music. I know if I had stayed in P.E. in high school, I would not have gotten through those first two years. However, I obviously couldn't do that with math. In my resource classes, they helped us out with our math homework every day. Math was a hard one for pretty much all of the kids and everyone definitely needed help. Lupe and Mrs. Byker were wonderful enough to make sure they understood the material in all of the classes, so they could help us out with it the best that they could. There was one time I needed help on a certain assignment and Mrs. Byker pulled out her dated copy of it from years earlier she kept in her binder. I looked at the date on the top and said, "I was in fifth grade when you did this paper!" She said, "We don't need to talk about that." She did the same for math and either she or Lupe would help out a whole group of us on our homework assignment.

When I was a sophomore, I was having an exceptional amount of trouble with my math class. I didn't understand hardly any of the material I was supposed to be learning, and I had a hard time staying focused when I was in class because I would just kind of give up on it. It didn't make any sense to me and I was becoming increasingly frustrated with it. However, I wouldn't be being completely honest if I didn't say that interest was also a factor. It kind of goes hand in hand with the communication. All of those conversations I have observed might have been about something I didn't have any interest in or I just didn't have anything to offer about whatever was being discussed. I think that is the case for a lot of people like me. If I know what the answer to a question is, or I have a lot of previous knowledge on it, I do a lot better having a conversation. I think the same can be said for my interest in math. I wasn't as interested in the subject, so I didn't have as easy of a time staying focused on it. I finally voiced my frustrations, but they weren't really understood the way I meant them to be understood. The moral of the story was that I didn't like the feeling of being in a class and not knowing anything. I didn't like having a paper in front of me in class I didn't know how to even get started on while everyone else sitting at my table was working on it on their own. I also had been called on by my math teacher to solve a problem I obviously did not know how to solve. He had gotten the beginning-of-the-year paper I wrote to all of my teachers, but he hadn't learned all of our names yet. He had a random name generator set up on his computer to select one of us to call on to answer a question, and he didn't realize he wasn't supposed to call on me when my name popped up on there. I always get so tense when teachers randomly call on people because I am always prepared for the worst. The kids at my table actually helped me out that day and I was able to get through it, but it still affected me whenever something like that happened.

I was always concerned about situations such as that. At this point, I feel like I am so good at picking up on cues and knowing when something is going to happen. There was a time in college where I just had the feeling my teacher was going to call on me, so I conveniently slipped out the door to the bathroom and I heard her say my name right after I left. I am one step ahead of those types of situations because of how many times those things have happened to me. Allison was in one of my classes where a substitute called on me once, and she told me after class that she thought the beginning of the song "London Bridge" (clean version) by Fergie was going through everyone else's minds. If you haven't heard that song, it starts out with the words "Oh Snap!" and "Get ready for this!" while police sirens play in the background. Most of the kids in my classes went to school with me all the way up, and they all knew that, for whatever reason, I didn't have to do or say anything in front of the class. I think they all probably did have something like that going through their heads while my mind was racing with thoughts of panic whenever something like that happened.

A lot of my struggles with math can be attributed to the fact I need to be able to picture things. When I read a book, I put faces of people I actually know on the characters. If it describes a character as someone with red hair and freckles, for example, I will think of someone in my life who somewhat matches that description and I will use them as my picture. I will create my own vision of the setting in my head based on the description of it in the book as well. I take something that, for other people, is open-ended, and I put my own twist on it in my mind so I can understand it. If I am unable to picture it, I won't understand it. In fifth grade, I had to read a historical book, and I scored poorly on the test we took when we were done with it. As a result, I had to read the book again, and my mom worked very diligently with me to make sure I understood it a little bit better. The next time, I was able to score higher on the test. In that particular situation, the book was hard for me to understand because it was based in a time frame I obviously can't picture very well, and it used words that I didn't know the meaning of. It referenced things I just didn't have pictures of in my head. For example, the whole time I was reading it, I thought the word "redcoat" was literally a red coat, so that is what I was picturing in my mind. I was not thinking of a soldier at all. There was another time where we played a game in my history class and we were taking turns answering questions. When it was my turn, the question was, "What is women's suffrage?" I said, "Women suffering," and then my partner banged his head on his desk. Because of the way I get confused with words like that sometimes, it makes it difficult to complete assignments when I am not clear on what is being asked of me.

The fact that I didn't have anything to picture was the reason I think I had such a hard time understanding math. If anything, I understood it more if there was a diagram or a graph because that gave me something to picture in my mind. I remember working with Mrs. Byker one on one at some point during the school year. I was grateful for that experience because I think the outside noises and the other students sometimes had more of an effect on my focus than I even realized at the time. Also, when I am working one on one with a teacher like that, I am able to ask questions and make sure I am getting the information the way that is best understood by me. When I am in a group setting, I won't raise my hand and ask a question if I don't understand something. I am too embarrassed to do so, but when I am working one on one with a teacher, I am a lot more confident in doing that.

Sometimes, if I didn't understand an assignment that was too vague, I just wouldn't ever finish it or turn it in. Most of the time, I would never say anything about it either. Then, my list of missing work would just keep piling up and piling up, and my grades would be dropping lower and lower, until I eventually had to face the music and get the work done. When I was going through a time where I was having a lot of anxiety towards school, I was significantly bad in this way. My mom always told me she wasn't as worried about grades as she was me just making it to school everyday. I think she didn't want to put even more pressure on me when there was already so much, and she wanted to focus on making sure that I was comfortable. She was supportive and understanding of me in this way and she knew, when a teacher would tell her in a meeting that I hadn't turned any papers in for weeks, to check my backpack because usually it was there. Typically, there was something standing in the way of me turning in the work.

There were a lot of times when I didn't want to turn in my math homework because I only had half of it done. When talking to other students, I would hear my teachers say things like, "Don't bother to turn it in if it isn't completed. It will automatically be a zero." What I wasn't understanding was that those kinds of rules didn't necessarily apply to me. They were able to give me more leeway than they would give most other students, but hearing those words said to other kids made me scared to turn in my half-completed work. My teacher told me once, "Seven out of ten is better than zero out of ten," and then I handed him about forty missing assignments. There was another time where my teacher had changed the way he had his students turn in work. There was a new basket on the opposite side of the room than the one we had originally turned in our work at. I was never going to ask, "Hey, where do I turn this in?" Instead, I would just let it sit in my backpack while my grades dropped. Sometimes, the reason for my bad grades were just simple communication barriers such as that.

When I look back on how I communicated with people when I was in school, it bothers me. I have always known that autism usually causes a person to struggle socially, but I never really thought that applied to me. I didn't notice my differences in terms of social interaction until I was out of school. I attributed most of it to my personality. However, I feel like now I am able to recognize the areas in which I can improve socially, and it makes me wish I had noticed it in high school. My quietness, my inability to start the conversation, and my body language make me come off as someone who doesn't want to talk to you when I actually would love to. When I say body language, I mean my habit of folding my arms, eye contact, and just kind of staring at people as they engage in a conversation I am trying to be a part of. I fold my arms because it makes me more comfortable. I don't know what else to do with them and it is just something I have always done. Sometimes, I just disengage altogether and I excuse myself from social situations. I feel like I have gotten worse at eye contact, but it really just might be I am more aware of it now. I won't look at people in the eye for more than a couple seconds when I am having a conversation with them. I do something with my hands, I pretend to fix my hair, I bite my nails like crazy, or I find a place to look that isn't the other person's face. That is what one on one conversations are like for me.

On the contrary, I have realized as I have gotten older, I stare at people inappropriately sometimes. That is when I am not having a direct conversation with the person. I used to tell my mom that the boy I liked would stare at me and my mom used to say, "Were you staring at him first?" I would just go, "Of course not!" when I knew that was definitely what was happening. Sometimes, I was just analyzing people. Sometimes, I was trying a little bit too hard to make eye contact with them. A lot of times, I was doing my rope in my head to what people were saying and that would make my eyes kind of fixate on them as I rubbed my fingers together. (Weird, I know!) My quietness was typically also a result of doing my rope in my head or just simply not knowing what to say or how to say it. However, my fear of conversations also played a major role in my quietness. I have had a conversation with someone before where I asked them a yes or no question and they replied with, "Cool!" I immediately knew they hadn't been listening to me and I wondered, "Do I sometimes do that to other people without realizing it?" I am sometimes so wrapped up in my own head that my mind wanders as people are talking to me and I don't mean to seem like I'm not listening, but I could see where that happens occasionally. Sometimes, it just takes me awhile to warm up to a new person or situation.

I was once introduced to someone and, upon shaking her hand, I just smiled at her. There used to be some normal social interaction words I was incapable of saying and I really mean that. I don't know why, but it was like my brain just would not let me say those words. It was almost like they sparked more of an opportunity for further social interaction and I wasn't interested in furthering my interaction. One of them was, "How are you?" When people would ask me how I was, I would just say, "Good," and that was the end of the conversation. I remember asking my mom once, "If you are having a bad day, are you supposed to say 'Bad'? Because I never say 'bad', even when I am doing bad." Now, I still just tell them that I am good, but I am able to say, "How are you?" back to them afterwards. Another sentence I could never manage to make myself say was, "Nice to meet you." When this lady shook my hand and told me it was nice to meet me, she was obviously expecting me to say it back. Instead, I just shook her hand and smiled. I couldn't give her the response she wanted because, for whatever reason, I couldn't say it. She looked me square in the eye and said, "Do you speak?" It really insulted me when she said that. Here I am constantly struggling with having conversations with people the right way, and she just kind of, without realizing it, rubbed it in my face that I was doing a bad job. With that being said, there have been times where I have met people, and I have immediately felt like I could talk to them, but that does not happen very often at all. As a result, I am kind of left depending on other people to help me out here and I am starting to realize that, a lot of times, they won't. It's on me.

Sometimes, I feel like I take huge strides in areas I have struggled with for years and something happens that has the ability to send me right back to the beginning. When I was a senior, I had talked myself into participating in a socratic seminar for one of my classes. It was an assignment I could have gotten out of, but we all thought it was important that I keep working on speaking in front of people. It was basically just half of my class sitting in a circle discussing an important topic we were assigned to discuss while the other half of the class sat back and watched. Then, you switched places with each other. I went in confident that I was going to do it. I had practiced, I had all of my notes ready, I was prepared to say exactly what I thought, and I found my seat in the circle. That was big in itself that I even sat down in the circle. I put my hands underneath my legs because it made me a little bit more comfortable, and I was also able to regulate how much I was nervously doing with my hands. When everyone else got to class, there were too many people in the circle and my teacher said that someone had to get out. One of the kids yelled, "Nose goes!" and I tried to get my hands out from under my legs, but it was too late. I was the last one to put my finger on my nose and thus I got kicked out of the circle. When they switched, I was too upset to go back in. Sometimes, I just wish that people could understand how things like that will mess me up. They will throw me for a complete loop. Other kids might not care, but it will affect me. I had been working hard to even sit down in the circle so I applauded myself later for at least doing that, but I was frustrated because I had wanted to do more.

I saw my peers talking in the microphone at the rallies, speaking out whenever they had something to say, and being noticed by other people. My brothers were actively involved in sports all year round. They were always doing something and they were good at it. My sister played a few sports, but she also participated in a lot of musical theater productions. I didn't do anything. I have been to so many football games in my life and I still don't even get it. I have been to lots of Shakespeare plays and I always have to read a synopsis to know what is going on. I had people ask me when I got to high school, "What sports do you play?" I would just have to say, "I don't like sports." One time, I tried to be funny and say something like, "What are sports?" but then it just turned into a very awkward social encounter. I had someone keep asking me once, "What about singing?" (My sister Lindsey is also a great singer). I told them that, no, I didn't sing. I know all of the lyrics to hundreds of songs, but you don't want to hear me try to sing them for the sake of your ears. Lindsey and I will have "riff-offs" from time to time where we take turns singing a song and, when we hear a certain word, we jump in with a new song. It is like a contest of being able to match lyrics of different songs, but Lindsey always jumps in with, "Oh my goodness!

Your tone! It's way off!" And I just yell at her, "It's not a singing competition!!" My siblings actually all have their own levels of social anxiety, but they are three people I look up to and love with all my heart. I have always compared myself to other people and I still struggle with this a lot. I feel like I am constantly behind everyone else. I just give myself a pat on the back for having decent social interactions when they happen. You know you're autistic when you come home and say, "Wow. What a great social day!" I am still having to learn to remind myself that comparing myself to others is pointless. I am in my own unique situation and I am still learning and growing with every step I take.

Chapter Fifteen: The Drop Of A Hat

People with autism can and will accomplish great things. You just have to take it one step at a time and not worry too much about falling behind.

In the middle of my sophomore year, my mom got a text from Molly. She is the speech therapist at the elementary school I went to when I was little, and her kids went to preschool with me. She was interested in meeting with me and wanted my mom's permission to do so. She had been at a conference and learned about a certain curriculum she wanted to try out with me. She knew about me because she knew my mom and hearing about this curriculum made her think of me. Outside of her actual job, she meets with some older kids in the district whom she thinks she can help. It isn't part of her job. She just does it out of the kindness of her heart and she is amazing at it. After that first meeting in the middle of my sophomore year, we met with each other once a week for the rest of my high school career. Sometimes, she came to the high school and got me out of class. Other times, I went to the elementary school to her office once the school day was over. That was my favorite way to do it because we had an unlimited amount of time to talk. These meetings meant a lot to me because they were an opportunity to really open myself up to someone I trusted, explain my thoughts and feelings, and hear valuable feedback from someone who truly cared to help me. I started calling her my "social learning therapist" because that is what she is. She taught me all about social norms and whenever I told her a story we would walk through it, and analyze all of the social things that occurred.

When I was in high school, I had a few things happen to me that were bigger than something I could just come to a conclusion about in my head. I needed to talk it out with somebody. A lot of times, I won't necessarily realize what something means until I discuss it with someone else because they can interpret it a little better than I can. Those kinds of things will sometimes go over my head. I am a literal thinker and I always take what people say as the truth. When I was little, my mom would confront me about things and say, "How did this break?" I used to answer her by saying, "Do you want me to make something up or do you want me to tell you the truth?" Because I am a very honest person, I tend to just assume everyone else is the same way. I don't always pick up on the signs that someone is not being honest. When I was in junior high and high school, I used to have a terrible time ordering for myself at restaurants or paying for things at a store. The concept of giving money and getting change back used to really trip me up. I once ordered myself a meal at the fair that cost about five dollars and I handed the lady both of the twenties I had in my hand. She came back to the window and said, "Sweetie, you gave me way too much money." I used to even forget that getting money back was part of the process and I would walk away without my change on occasion. Even now, I sometimes get so nervous that I will not be thinking straight and I forget important things like that.

There are also a few incidents that happened where people used this trait against me and manipulated me. At dance team performances, we were all given a twenty dollar bill to buy ourselves something. I was ordering lunch with my classmate at the snack bar and she kept all of my change. I didn't even realize this was a bad thing. I had no idea it was happening because I just didn't understand the concept of how money worked. There was another time in high school where I went to lunch with a few kids in my grade. I had twenty dollars on me to spend and I was ordering something that was about four dollars total. I ended up also using it to buy one of the other kids his lunch, which cost about the same amount, because once we got there, he said he didn't have any money on him. When I got my change back, he handed me a couple of ones out of it and kept the rest. That completely went over my head, but when I got home that day, my mom asked me where my change was. When I showed her, she told me I should have a lot more change than what I had. I just have never understood dishonesty and I have a hard time noticing it.

There are some situations I don't know how to handle and there are some things that I, as an autistic person, can be a little bit more susceptible to than others. In certain situations, manipulation can be one of them. However, I am actually pretty good at knowing when someone's intentions are skewed and I can read people fairly well. The thing I struggle with is being too nice to people, even when I shouldn't be. I feel like I have spent my entire life conditioning myself to please people and be nice no matter what. I do think being kind is almost always the way to go. However, I have spent my whole life doing the absolute best I can to avoid any type of negative situations and, by doing that, I sacrifice myself in an almost unhealthy way. I will not stand up for myself. I will not assert myself and I will kind of just let people treat me in ways I shouldn't be treated. I have hardly ever expressed to someone they were upsetting me. I just let them do and say whatever they want and all that does is build up resentment in myself. It is probably my biggest problem with communication in terms of the close relationships I have had with people, but it is also something I struggle with in all interactions. I have had people try to get me to write their papers for them and, in the moment, I won't know what to do in that situation. I will probably give the hint that my answer is no, but I will not come right out and say it. As a result, someone else would have to get involved and take care of it for me. Because I am this way, I have been in situations where I have been nice to people who I shouldn't have even really engaged with in conversation.

There are also certain times where I have been in situations and I haven't known how to handle it. I was getting gas in my car alone recently and I was approached by someone who wanted to know if I had any money. It was an older woman and I just had the mindset I was going to give her a couple of dollars because I wanted to avoid the negative interaction of denying her money. I was standing right next to the passenger door of my car and I told her to let me check. Then, I turned my back to see if I had any money in my center console. Right when I did it, I immediately knew that turning my back was not a good choice because then she could have come up behind me. I just turned back really quick without actually looking for the money, and I told her I was sorry, but I didn't have any. In that situation, I ended up kind of being forced to have that interaction because I got a little bit freaked out at the alternative. Unless someone is very outwardly alarming, I don't see them as someone who could potentially be a danger to me. I don't read those kinds of situations very well and I don't always notice things that are happening around me.

There was one incident in high school that sticks in my mind where I was manipulated by my peers in a way that was mean. Toward the end of my sophomore year, I was in my room doing my rope late one night when my phone rang. There aren't very many things that can bring me out of that rope and music world and when they do, they have the potential of making me a little bit agitated. My grandma used to walk down to our house with a book to read when my parents weren't home just so I could continue doing my rope where I was the most comfortable. Nights spent in my room were essential to me. When my phone went off that night, it was a girl I went to school with who was a close friend of mine. She said, "Jillian, what is this all about?" She had a boy who she liked who also went to school with us, and she wanted to know why I was telling him a bunch of horrible things about her over text message. I was very confused and I had no idea what she was talking about.

I hadn't ever talked to him and I hardly knew him at all. However, he was talking to someone over text message who he thought was me because they told him they were me. I think they probably thought since I was friends with this girl, they could get information out of him, and they could say what they wanted about her and he would believe whatever they said. It worked and he confronted her about it by saying, "Your friend Jillian said this, this, and this about you." When she heard that, she subsequently confronted me about it. I ended up finding out who it was that was doing that and it was something that was really hard for me to process. I couldn't understand why someone would pretend to be me and I didn't like that it had put me in an awkward position with my friend. Even still, it is very confusing for me when I have someone tell me something to my face that contradicts with the things they say when other people are around. For example, I once had someone talk horribly about another person to me, but when that person was around, they acted as though they were great friends. That is a kind of behavior I am incapable of understanding. It just isn't a part of my personality.

I had a few experiences in high school I am grateful for that taught me so many things about myself and other people. When I was in middle school, I had a huge crush on a boy and this lasted a very long time. I used to drive my family nuts because it was all I talked about. Autistic people have what we call a "special interest." Many people with autism are especially interested in certain people, places, or subjects. A special interest can really be anything and a lot of autistic people know almost everything there is to know about their special interest. A crush and a special interest are not the same thing, but my special interests have always pertained to people. I get infatuated with certain people and I find out everything there is to know about said person. I even kind of mirror them in my life. For example, if someone I looked up to did their hair a certain way, I would want to copy them and do *my* hair that way. When I was younger, I was obsessed with Michael Jackson and I actually taught myself how to moonwalk. In my third grade school picture, I have on a yellow shirt and khaki pants, and my hair is in pigtails. I was obsessed with Bindi Irwin at the time and I wanted to dress exactly like her. Even now, I have to remind myself that I don't really want to dress or do my hair like a certain person. It is just my special interest coming out.

Because of this, when I was little and I had someone I thought was cute, that person would kind of develop into being a special interest of mine. I always had crushes on a few of my brothers' friends. I thought they were so cute and I wasn't afraid to say so. I remember once walking up to the top of the bleachers after one of Ethan's basketball games. (It was a real sacrifice for me to walk all the way up there!) His team was in a huddle right next to the bleachers and I walked over to the edge and looked down at them. Then, I took off my hat and dropped it right in the middle of their huddle on purpose. They all looked, I blushed, and then I said, "Hey, Cole! You want to hand me my hat?" When I knew the boys had friends coming over, I would write love notes on my portable white board and leave it where I knew they would see it. It would say things like, "Hi, Joey. I think you're hot." I used to write them on the asphalt with sidewalk chalk if I knew they were going to go outside to play basketball. I once spelled it out with my magnetic alphabet letters on our fridge. I was a very weird child and Ethan and Austin didn't think I was very funny.

During my junior and senior years of high school, I had a boyfriend and the experience of that was very valuable to me. We dated for nearly two years and I learned a lot about what works and what doesn't work in terms of a relationship for me as an autistic person. My biggest hardship was the fact that I am always afraid to say things. I am not good at communicating things with people. I won't tell somebody when something is wrong. I don't confide in people very easily, and I don't really always know how to say what I am feeling in a kind, yet efficient way. I can either be too nice and not efficient enough to feel successful in getting my point across, or I am too efficient and not kind enough to have handled it successfully. Even though this fact is true about me, there were times where I did tell him about what I was feeling and he was always receptive to it. Getting to know his family was a huge step for me in terms of my social interaction. I grew a lot from it, I saw a major change in myself, and I am grateful for the experience. Once we got out of high school, we weren't seeing each other very much. We had very different busy schedules and neither of us really knew how to fit each other in. After a long day, I need to do my rope and my music for a certain length of time and that sometimes got in the way of me ever asking him to do something after the day was done. We both needed time to ourselves, we were getting used to such a different phase in our lives, and it wasn't the right time to have a relationship. We had a really good conversation about it and we both kind of opened ourselves up to each other in ways we hadn't ever done.

One of the things I always worry about with relationships is the fact that I have autism. I worry about how that can affect a relationship I might have in the future. In this case, we had gone to school together forever, and he knew that I had autism. I worry about future times where people won't know and I will have to explain it to them. I don't know whether that is something that should be talked about in the beginning or if it should be something I talk about further into a relationship. I worry that it could be a deal breaker for some people and that scares me. It is a disability that gives me hardships people can't see and I can see where it could be confusing to someone. My rope and music are also something I worry about because they are so secretive and strange. How will I ever explain that I twirl a rope, make a noise, pace back and forth with headphones on while I'm locked in my room for hours upon hours? Of course, a relationship is also something that requires a lot of responsibility and time, and while it is something I want to try again someday, I think I have some more growing and learning about myself to do first.

It is a very hard thing for me to open up about my autism. I don't necessarily like having to come out and talk about it in conversations with people. If someone asks me a question, that is one thing, but I never bring up my autism when I talk to people. That is why I worry about things like this. I worry about it with future jobs. I don't know why the thought of saying the words, "I have autism," is so difficult for me to think about, but it is. I am getting a lot of practice with it in college. It hasn't been easy, but it is necessary in order for me to be able to get what I need. My family always tells me, "The people that matter don't care," and I try to remember that every time I have to introduce my disability to someone.

Back in eighth grade, I made a post on Instagram and Facebook about my autism. It had been a secret my entire life. I had always been embarrassed and ashamed of it. I never wanted anyone to know it was something that I dealt with. I think that what fueled this fire in me to post about it was the fact I was having such a horrible time in P.E. I knew a lot of my peers were seeing me cry constantly and I knew they didn't understand. I wanted to try to give them an opportunity to understand, so I decided to open myself up in that way and be honest with my peers about what I was struggling with. To me, it seemed better to let them know why I was crying every day instead of constantly worrying about what they might be thinking. I stared at my phone for two hours that night with my finger hovering over that button. Finally, I went ahead and pressed it.

When I posted it, I didn't get very much feedback from my peers, but the small amount I did get was good and it made me feel inspired to do even more. I created a blog, which I kind of fell out of, and now I have a Facebook page where I share what is going on in my life in terms of my autism and what I am learning along the way. At this point, I have typed the word autism into my phone so many times that whenever I am trying to write my brother Austin's name, it automatically corrects it to autism. I end up sending a text that says, "What are you up to today, Autism?" (Sometimes, I do wonder what it's up to!) When I created that first post, I said, "This is me and I'm not ashamed of it. My autism doesn't define me. I define my autism." It was a quote from Alexis Wineman, who I actually got to meet at a conference my freshman year, along with Temple Grandin. I don't know if I really agree with it that much anymore because I feel like my autism has held me back from so many things in my life. However, I have pushed beyond it a lot too.

There are a lot of hardships in the world of autism, but there are a lot of wonderful things about it as well. And, maybe before I worry about finding someone who will accept me for who I am, I need to make sure I am doing that myself. I think I am, but I always have room for improvement. There are times where I kind of feel glad nobody in my college classes knows about my autism. At least, as far as I know, they don't. It feels like I have a clean slate as opposed to high school. However, it doesn't really matter because there are people out there who will give me a chance, no matter how much they know about me. It isn't something to be ashamed of and that is something I have had to learn. Even though my autism has held me back many times, I do ultimately define what effect my autism has on me in terms of my mindset. I can dwell on the fact that there are things I cannot do, or I can spend a lot of time working towards being able to accomplish my goals in my own time and at my own pace.

Chapter Sixteen: Step On It

There are many different perceptions in this world. Don't let them define you. Speak your wisdom and teach instead.

One thing I never really thought I was going to be able to do was drive a car. I had a few reasons for this. One was the simple fact I was awful at driving anything. I had driven my grandpa's four-wheeler in our orchard once and I crashed into a tree. I pressed the gas too hard with my foot and hadn't turned the handlebars enough to avoid missing it. I also ran a golf cart into a pole once when I was riding around with Allison at *her* grandparents' house. That time, I hadn't understood the concept of the brakes, and I just took my foot off of the gas pedal instead. Actually, both times, I didn't really understand the brakes. I was in elementary school, so I was definitely a lot better once I reached driving age. Those incidents just scared me into thinking I was not going to drive a car. I thought I would not be able to react quickly. The other reason had to do with my music. This problem was easier to solve, but it still worried me. I thought I wouldn't be able to drive and have the radio on at the same time. I was worried that my mind would start to go into that rope/music world, which would be very dangerous. I made a rule I was never going to drive with music on. However, I learned I am able to regulate this, and I can have the music on at a low volume when I drive. Once I got to age fifteen, I knew driving was something I wanted to try. My dad taught me how to drive in his work truck and I absolutely loved driving. We drove around the back roads, the fairgrounds parking lot, and the frontage road right near our house. I wanted to drive all the time, and I really loved the challenge of it. I still love driving.

I did driver's education class through school at the end of my freshman year and then I got my permit. I did a bunch of practice tests on the computer and I felt really prepared for it. Before I could get my license, I had to do some behind-the-wheel training with a driving instructor. My school provided this also, but in order to do it through them, I would have to drive with a few other kids at the same time because they did the training in groups. That made me very nervous; I didn't want to have to do that. Instead, we found a driving school in a town about a half an hour away and I signed up. It met the same requirements and I met with the instructor individually, which was what I definitely preferred to do. I had only ever driven on back roads, yet she took me on the freeway within the first few minutes. I was not accustomed to driving fast. Ask anyone who has ever ridden in the car with me. I am a speed limit person. I thought forty miles an hour was super fast since that was about as fast as I had ever driven.

When we merged onto the freeway, my instructor yelled at me, "Do you want to die?!" I took her literally and said, "Well, no. Not right now." She said, "Then, step on it!" She freaked me out, so I sped all the way up to eighty, and she had to tell me to slow down. After I did my lessons with her, I got my license in February of my sophomore year. My parents didn't allow me to drive to school until my junior year began. I was still having such a hard time making it onto campus in the mornings and I needed my mom to drop me off. If she hadn't, I probably would have driven there and never walked in or even left when I wasn't supposed to. I think that was my parents' way of making sure that didn't happen and they didn't give me that freedom until I was able to prove I could handle it. The summer after sophomore year, I had to go to summer school for a week to make up for some biology credits I was missing. I was so mad I had to do this, but my mom used it as good practice for getting myself to school by allowing me to drive to summer school. Once my junior year began, I was driving myself to school every day. I picked out a certain parking spot I liked and I went there every morning. My grandpa spent seven months fixing up my cousin Natalie's old car for me to drive. He put lots of time and money into it, and it was ready just in time for my seventeenth birthday.

I worried about getting pulled over for any reason at all. I drive as cautiously as I can, but I still get very nervous whenever I see a cop on the road. I did a mock pullover with Molly so I could see what it would actually be like if I did get pulled over. I was able to ask the officer questions about what I should do and it was a very helpful experience for me. While I still don't want to get pulled over, it helps me to know what to expect. Along with the mock pullover, Molly and I decided to make a card for me and I keep it tucked into my sun visor. It has my name on it and it explains my autism. In the situation I did get pulled over, it is possible I could get very upset and meltdown. I can see that happening very easily and this card is meant to help me if it does. It is for me to hand someone in a pullover or an accident and let them know my information. It says I may not respond to questions, I may be overly emotional, and I may seem as though I am being uncooperative. Autism gets misunderstood very easily and when tensions are already high, it can be detrimental. After it explains everything, it has some of my family members' phone numbers on it who I know would be around if needed. I haven't used this card for any reason yet, but it gives me a sense of peace knowing I have it with me. Driving can make for a lot of sticky situations and it makes me feel a lot more comfortable knowing I have this card with me just in case anything were to happen.

My junior and senior years were remarkably better than any of my previous years of school. From second grade to my sophomore year, I had so many barriers, misunderstandings, and anxieties that I didn't enjoy school. I actually love to learn, to be challenged, and to have structure and a routine, but my other issues were much more prominent in my life. I couldn't shake the bad stuff and it overshadowed all of the good stuff. My autism basically ruled my life for all of those years of school, and I will always deal with issues caused by my autism. That is never going to go away. However, it becomes easier. It got a whole lot easier for me once I had a better understanding of myself. It took years and it was hard to come by, but it was so magnificent to me when I wasn't plagued by it anymore. My junior and senior years were absolutely wonderful, and I am so thankful I was able to finally experience school without all of that chronic anxiety. There were still some situational things that would upset me or make me nervous, but for the most part, I was perfectly fine. If it hadn't happened that way, I can't say I would be in college right now. Probably not. Why would I be going to school when I didn't have to? There was a time where I never expected to be living life the way I am right now. I am a working student. When I think about it, that is kind of insane because I was what seemed to be a lost cause. I felt helpless and I never saw myself getting to do all of the things I have done, but I have surprised myself a lot of times along the way.

Driving actually deserves some of the credit. While it was worrisome for my parents, I actually think knowing I had the ability to leave school if I really needed to brought me comfort. There were a few times I did go out to my car and leave if I was having a super hard time, but I wasn't doing it sneakily. If I left, people knew that I was leaving. I was able to drive myself to lunch, and sometimes I took that time to go home for a few minutes if I needed some downtime. My dad's jobsite was only a few blocks away and I went there for lunch quite a few times as well. He is a construction foreman and his job sites are typically in another town. However, during my junior and senior years, he was working on a project just down the road from my school, which was also very helpful and comforting for me. My brother Austin was working in town also and I asked him to meet me for lunch every once in awhile. I just think that knowing I had the option to go if I had to was something that was always in the back of my mind, and it gave me a sense of comfort when I didn't even realize it.

Another thing that really gave me a good break both of those years was a class I took called Careers With Children. It was right up my alley. I have always loved working with children and it is something that I aspire to do in the future. I have pretty much admired my teachers since I was in preschool. The calendars, pointers, chalkboards, and everything in between fascinated me, and I knew I wanted to be a teacher one day. This class gave me such great classroom experience, which was amazing to have. It had its own curriculum, but we spent most of the time working in a classroom at the nearby elementary school, Mill Street.

It lasted for two class periods, which meant I was there for a couple of hours at a time. It was so much fun to form relationships with the kids, get to do teacher work, and just see how a classroom is run. I worked in a kindergarten class and the teacher was Mr. Texara's wife. She is an amazing teacher and I learned a lot from her. Besides being in the classroom, it was a great opportunity for me to decompress, and I think that is one of the main reasons why my last two years of school were so successful.

When I was working at Mill Street, I had a few experiences that stick out in my mind. One spring afternoon during my senior year, I only had one class left to attend once I got back to school. The schedule at my high school rotated. If we had periods 1,2,3,4,5 on one day, then the next day, we would have 6,7,1,2,3. Then, 4,5,6,7,1 and so on. Because of the rotating schedule, each class was at a different time every day, and there were some days where we didn't have a certain class at all. On this particular day, I had Careers With Children the periods before and after lunch, which meant I only had one class left. It was in April and the elementary school actually dedicated a lot of that month to teaching kids about autism. They learn about the kinds of things autistic children might do, such as flapping their hands, and they talk about how you should treat the kids who do those things. I thought it was great to hear Mrs. Texara talk to the kids about autism and it was very cute to hear their responses. When I went to school there, they did not do all of this during the month of April. Now that people are learning more and more about autism, we are seeing it in more children, and it is something that probably all of the kids in that class will be around at some point. Actually, they were around it right at that moment because I was sitting in the room with them. They only knew me as their high school helper, but unbeknownst to them, they were talking about the kind of child I had been just a few years prior at that same school.

After they had this talk, Mrs. Texara told me about the balloon release they were going to have a little while later. The entire school went out onto the field together and everyone was given a baby blue balloon to set free. She asked me if I wanted to stay and I knew I wanted to, but I didn't want to have to be late to class. However, she knew my next period teacher pretty well, and she called him to ask if I could stay a few extra minutes. I did get to release my own balloon that day. I was overwhelmed with gratitude I was able to be there. There were hundreds of blue balloons that the kids let off and it was beautiful. I remember thinking I had once been there at that school, frightened and alone, never really knowing how I was going to feel or whether or not I was going to have a good day. It was my old stomping grounds paying tribute and showing their respect for people just like me, and it meant so much to me to be able to witness that.

I ended up working at Mill Street a lot during my senior year. In the fall, I enrolled in a youth employment program. I worked on a resume, application, cover letter, interview, and many other things that pertain to getting a job. Then, after all of that was completed, I was able to actually get one. This class was provided through my high school and it was so wonderful to be able to have that experience. These are all things that don't come naturally to me like they do to others and having a class to teach me all of the ins and outs of getting a job was very helpful. I ended up working at Mill Street, but for the after school program. I basically did whatever was asked of me, which was supervising the kids, helping with projects and homework, and watching the door. Parents had to come to a locked door and knock when they were there to pick up their child and there were a lot of days where I opened it, let them in, and called for the child over the walkie-talkies. I was so nervous about that at first because people were going to be listening to me. When I am nervous, I start to question everything about what I am doing, and I usually end up making a complete fool of myself. For example, when I was nervous about talking over the walkie-talkies, I couldn't figure out how to turn the walkie-talkie on. There were parents waiting for me and if I had just taken a breath and calmed down, I probably would have been able to figure it out a lot sooner. It also doesn't help if I know people are watching because it will add some insecure feelings and make me even more nervous. However, I did finally master the walkie-talkies.

When I was working at Mill Street, I had my first experience of seeing a child who reminded me of myself. Ever since then, I have met many children who reminded me of myself in different ways, but the first time was different for me because I hadn't ever experienced it before. I have always been pretty good at spotting autism in another person. I can almost sense it, even just seeing a stranger out somewhere. It's in the facial expressions, the body movements, the hand motions, and many other factors. Sometimes, I can just kind of tell and I wonder if people have ever done that with me. If anyone has ever noticed the way I twirl my fingers, have one earphone in at all times, or even the way I smile at them and turn my head away fast. It isn't visibly noticeable on the outside, but if you have that background knowledge, then it kind of becomes that way to you. One day, I had my back turned working on something with one of the kids and I heard a noise, but it wasn't just any noise. It was *my* noise. It was the same humming noise I have made with my rope every single day for as long as I can remember. It is a fairly normal sound and I had been tuning it out for awhile, just like everyone else around me was. However, there is something about the way the sound is repetitive and steady, and it only really stops when you have to breathe. It is deep and low and sounds a little bit like you're in pain. I instantly recognized it when I heard it.

When I turned around, a child behind me was staring at the wall and squeezing his fingers. There were pictures pinned up along the bottom of the wall at eye level with the kids, and this child's eyes were looking right into those pictures while he made the humming noise. It was probably just how I looked all of those years in a public setting minus the unexplained and abrupt movement I did while at home. It made sense to me and I just felt like I knew what I was seeing. I looked at all of these kids and had kind of been able to place them with my classmates. I would say, "Oh, I think this little girl is going to be like so and so when she is a teenager." When I saw this happen, I had seen someone that I could say was going to be like *me*. I didn't have much of a type. I was just a girl that went to school and hardly said or did anything, but had a rope to go home to. I wanted to run and tell someone, "I saw that kid doing their rope!" but then I realized that nobody else knows what a rope is because I am the only one who calls it that. I have even done that before while looking through the pictures in my head. I have almost said out loud to people, "What picture was I on?" Then, I have had to stop myself from actually asking that question because it isn't a normal thing for most people. Sometimes, I almost forget not a lot of people think the way I do, which makes seeing someone doing the things I do pretty special to me.

When graduation came along, I was excited, but scared at the same time. I knew I wanted to go to college, but I knew my life was going to change drastically. I had to prepare myself to do more voicing and advocating for myself, which I had always been afraid of and let everyone else take care of for me. I understood it was going to be harder than I had experienced in high school, but I felt okay with all of it. I was ready for that transition, even though I knew it was going to be difficult. I was determined not to let anything get in the way of finishing out the year strong and getting my diploma. I met with the principal, Mr. Perry, just a few days before graduation to talk about the plan. He was always very accommodating and understanding of me. He did whatever he could to make sure I was comfortable and successful at his school. It was obvious he cared about his students. Mr. Texara was also someone who always fought for me and never gave up on me. If I was him, I would have. But he never did and I always knew he cared about me. No matter what the situation was, he was willing to talk to me about it and offer the best advice he could. There were many other adults I felt like I had valuable relationships with who were helpful and kind to me and all of them prepared me for what I would experience in college.

When he met with me a few days before graduation, he showed me the script that he and the vice principal would be reciting. I got to see when my name would be called and exactly how everything would go. He asked me how much of a percentage I would give as to if I was going to be able to get through graduation or not and I said, "100%." I was not going to let anything get in the way. When I promoted from eighth grade, they decided if I got too nervous to walk, I could just sit down next to my English teacher who was behind the stage. The principal planned to turn around during the ceremony when he got to my name to see if I was there, and if I wasn't, he would skip over my name. However, I was there and he did say my name. None of that needed to happen when I graduated from high school. I ended up being able to sit with people whom I was the most comfortable with. In eighth grade, we were assigned our partners and I had been next to great people, but it did make it easier in high school to be next to people who were close to me. In eighth grade, I didn't look out at the crowd once. I just looked at my feet. This time, I searched the crowd and I waved at my family. I was proud of myself, but I was sad at the same time. I had spent so many years terrified of school and using up all of my energy to stay away from it. Now, it was over and I had ended it with two wonderful years.

Graduation was just the best it could have possibly been, and when I walked across the stage, Mr. Perry gave me a high five. I remember thinking that him giving me a high five probably showed I was one of the kids who took a lot of work and had a hard time. However, I did take a lot of work and I did have a hard time, but I finally made it through, and he was a big part of the reason I did. I got to walk across the same stage on the same football field that my sister and my brothers got to walk across, and with the people I had been going to school with since kindergarten. I was so thankful for that.

During my first month as a college student, I met with the person who helped me set up my accommodations with my professors. He showed me how to do it at this meeting, and then it was easy enough that I have done it myself every semester since. I am glad because I left that meeting in tears. I had been asked a little bit insensitively about the things I dealt with in high school that were on my records. I didn't feel exactly comfortable confiding in somebody I had just met about those things, and I also felt a little bit judged about it. I realized I was now in a position where I was on my own. I wasn't going to have a resource teacher to fall back on. I already kind of knew that, but it really hit me when I left that meeting. Now, I would say that hasn't been the problem I thought it was going to be at all.

In March of my second semester, I had a group presentation I had continuously put off and put off. I knew I had to tell my group members about my autism and I was scared. I had worked out that I would not be presenting with my teacher, but it was up to me to work it out with my group members separately. I had three other classes to focus on at the same time and as my stress increased about one class, my performance in all of my other classes lowered significantly. Eventually, I had a huge meltdown right in the middle of the parking lot as I was running to my car. A small situation had come up in one of my night classes, and because I was so agitated about my group project in my other class, it threw me completely over the edge. It was bound to happen one way or another.

My parents had to come all the way to get me that night because I was too inconsolable to drive home, and I had also abandoned all of my stuff in the classroom when I left. It was the first time I had hit a really rough patch in college, and this is a time where I am so incredibly grateful that I have my mom. She is my biggest source of comfort. When something bad happens, all I want to do is tell my mom. When anything good happens, all I want to do is tell my mom. Before I make any form of a decision, I always want to see what my mom has to say first. When I talk to her, it is equivalent to talking to myself when nobody is listening. I am vulnerable, honest, open, comfortable, and accepted. I just let it all out. She gets to see that glimpse into my world and my mind that nobody else gets to see when I am just having a normal conversation with them. I have started to realize I don't ever feel better unless I let out my feelings either by crying or by talking to someone about it, which is typically my mom. I was able to send an apology email to my teacher and let my group members know I would not be presenting, but it was not without a ton of anxiety, pressure, and tears. I remember telling my mom I was just sick of it. I was tired of having to explain myself to people and having to apologize for being autistic. Right now, I am dreading the first week of my next semester because it calls for a ton of explanations to my new teachers. More times than not, people are so nice and receptive to what I have to say, but it is very daunting and tiresome for me to always be having to do that. It is one of the hard parts about being an autistic adult. Anytime my autism takes over, I feel like I have to explain it to everyone affected by whatever happened and it can be discouraging for me.

The one other difficult thing about college is time management. My rope and my music are essential to me, and when I am stressed, they are even more essential to me. This started to affect me during my first year of college because I would do my rope or my music instead of whatever assignment I should have been doing. If it stressed me out, I would put it off until I couldn't put it off any longer, which only made it even more stressful. I would use my rope and my music to take my mind off of school, and it would make me feel like I was always behind because I waited until the very last minute to get work done. In high school, I didn't have this problem because I had a class every year strictly meant for doing homework. In college, I don't have that option so it is up to me to get it done. However, when I have time, I typically want to spend it doing my rope and my music, so it has been a hard thing for me to learn how to balance. However, the thing I do like about college is the fact I can leave class unexplainably and nobody questions anything.

Typically, when I get nervous about something in class, I will walk out for a few minutes. If I am too nervous, I will leave completely, but most of the time, I try my hardest not to. I am in college to pass my classes, and I can only do that if I make it a priority to be there. In order to do this, I like to leave all of my stuff in the classroom when I walk out except my phone. I like to have my phone to call my mom and tell her what is happening. If I leave the rest of my stuff behind, I feel like I can't completely leave school. I have to trick myself into staying. If my stuff is in the classroom, I will have to go back because there are things that I need in there. If I brought it with me, I would see no reason to go back inside. This is one of the tricks I have learned to make sure that my autism and my barrier do not win because I am completely capable of going back inside and getting through college, even though I occasionally don't feel like I am.

The preschool my mom has worked at for almost ten years now expanded the year after I graduated high school, and I was offered one of the new teacher aide positions. It has been the most wonderful experience and just this last school year, I have had my very own teaching days! By watching how all of the kids interact with one another, I have realized something about myself. I started college to be a teacher in a classroom, but I don't know if I will be able to handle all of that work and responsibility. I know that isn't a positive way to look at it, but it might just be the way it is for me. I am not always able to handle too much stress and I know that. I know working with kids is where I am the happiest and that is what I want to pursue. I always look forward to my days spent at the preschool. I have never dreaded it once. The same can be said for when I worked at the elementary school. However, I have started to think I might try going for a job in occupational therapy or something along those lines. I have a passion for that because I was once the child receiving the help, and I know how much I loved having that experience. I am passionate about making sure that children who have disabilities or differences get their needs met because I know how extremely important it is. I also know how difficult it is to get through school when you're in that kind of position. Therefore, I feel like it is my calling to help children who come after me and I am going in that direction until I find something that sticks with me.

I was working on a project with a classmate once, and they were reiterating a story about someone else who they were annoyed with. Somewhere along the line they asked, "Are they autistic or something? Why can't they just answer the question?" I was kind of taken aback and it felt like they had punched me in my gut. Autism was used as an insult and I didn't like that very much. I knew that it wasn't an educated perception because it was wrong. Another time shortly after that, I was having a conversation with someone in my English class. We were in the middle of reading the book *Forrest Gump* and we were talking about our thoughts on the book. They said, "How can he join the army if he is autistic?" I said, "Huh?" They said, "Forrest Gump. He is highly autistic. Why would they let him in the army?" This comment surprised me for a lot of reasons, and it affected me a lot more than the first comment. We read that book as a class over the course of the next few weeks, and a lot of people would say things about what an idiot Forrest Gump was. After I had that conversation, whenever something like that was said about Forrest Gump, it hurt me. It made me sad. This perception was not educated either, in more ways than one, but it just hurt my feelings. Even though those perceptions were wrong, I didn't like that they even existed. Unfortunately, they are a part of the harsh reality autistic people and their families have to deal with.

Those people didn't know their comments were hurtful, but it shows there is work to be done. I was sitting in another class once and my group was talking about a person who I knew had autism. They said, "He only thinks of himself and he throws big fits." Another person said, "Are those the symptoms of autism?" They replied, "Yup." Then, someone brought up a picture of this person on their phone and showed it to the person sitting next to them. They said, "Oh my gosh. He doesn't even look like he has autism." That same person also told me I didn't look Mexican once when I said that I was Catholic. A lot of people with autism will tell you they don't like it when someone says that they don't look autistic. I kind of chalk it up to someone who doesn't know what autism is, so it doesn't necessarily offend me, but it is annoying at the same time. Autism doesn't have a look. It's in the characteristics you will start to notice it and every one of us is so different from the next. Though I do think there are similarities, there are definitely a lot of differences. I can hold a conversation, but there are a lot of underlying struggles that go along with that. I can write a book. I also have a rope that takes over my life. I don't know if I will ever be able to live alone. I would probably burn my new house down on the first night. If not the first night, definitely within the first week. There are a lot of things autistic people won't be able to do individually, but there are tons of things they will be able to overcome.

I met a mom a couple years ago who had a great perspective. She said, "He might not ever drive a car, but that's okay. We will always work towards it. He might not ever get married, but that's okay. We will always work towards it." My mom has always had the same perspective about me. There are many things my mom thought that I may not ever do, but she always worked towards it and now I can do those things. This is why I compare autism to being like a flower. We all have lots of growing to do and we all need help from other people. It will take a lot of work. A lot of watering, a lot of tending to, and a lot of sunshine. It might take longer than most. We will grow and then wilt a little bit. Then, it will take extra work to get us back where we need to be. We might be the last one in the patch, but in the end, we all blossom and we are all beautifully made up of our own shapes, sizes, and colors. Everyone blossoms at their own pace and in their own ways. For some of us, blossoming would be being able to live on our own, and for others, it might be being able to leave the house without assistance. Some of us might not be able to ride a bike until we are twelve and others may do it at six. Some might still be unable to at sixteen, but that's okay because you can always work towards it. I would say that I didn't fully feel like a blossomed flower until my junior year of high school, but I have even blossomed so much since then in many ways. For me, it is a matter of making sure that I stay that way. You can't stop working and you can't stop watering. There will always be ways I will be blossoming, and I still need to give myself that care and attention to ensure that I do. If you feel like you aren't going anywhere right now, keep trying and you will get there. You can always work towards it and, by doing that, you will blossom in your own way and at your own pace.

My first semester of college, I had a psychology class and we watched a documentary on perceptions of autism. My teacher was also autistic and he felt passionately about it, so he showed the class this video. After I watched it, I ended up making a post on social media about it. It just sparked a lot of thoughts and feelings in me and I felt like I had something to say. There were people in this documentary who thought very negatively about autism and had perceptions that were offensive to people like me. I think part of blossoming is being able to look past all of those perceptions and understand that having autism is not a bad thing. It makes you who you are. You offer things to the world other people don't and you have a way of seeing the world that is unique to you and only you. To me, that is pretty special. However, I definitely did not always feel like I do now. I still have moments where I wish I could experience at least one day without autism, but I understand this is who I am and I don't want to change. This documentary opened up feelings for me that were difficult to sift through, but the overall message was hopeful. After seeing it, I wanted people to know how I felt about the topic of perceptions of autism so I wrote this:

Friday, September 28, 2018

Perceptions

In one of my classes this week, we watched a documentary on the many different perspectives of what autism means and what autism looks like. Hearing some of the things that were said sent a sinking feeling to my gut and I was left with emotions that I have too often had to sift through. I was uncomfortable when I knew we would be watching this documentary because, if I'm being honest, I have let these twisted perceptions fill me with shame and embarrassment about an aspect of my life that will never go away and will always be a part of who I am. I knew this video would bring up these emotions for me and I prepared myself.

I often think back on things that happened to me when I was younger and all I feel is shame. I cringe and I immediately tell myself to think about something else. I can't say for sure, but I think one of the reasons I feel this way is because I know that people didn't understand. I know that people probably thought I was crazy or weird or unstable and just getting special treatment from those who were kind enough not to think that way about me. I mean, why wouldn't people have those thoughts? I look fine, I can talk, I can walk, I can take care of myself, and

I can have a conversation with you. But that has been the biggest battle I have had to fight.

People don't see that it takes everything in me to look at them in the eyes and talk to them, even though intimate conversations are probably one of my favorite things and all I want to do is have them with ease. They don't see the intense fear I have of new and different situations. People don't realize that taking care of myself is a huge task as I have the constant urge to be other places and do other things that my brain is pulling me towards at all times. And I can only push that feeling away for so long. They don't see the ticking time bomb in me when I go on vacation with my family and have to fight those feelings off. And they don't see the explosion when it all gets to be too much. And I never talk about it. Ever.

The people that made insensitive comments to me didn't know that I walked off campus not remembering the hour it took me to walk onto it. They didn't know that during that hour, my emotions took over my better judgment and I watched myself do and say things I never thought I would. And that was really me during those times. Even I thought I was crazy. There was something I really needed to say, some sort of anxiety that was making me freeze up, something I needed help to get myself through, something really bothering me, and I just couldn't say it. I couldn't express it. So instead I lost the ability to hide my disability and I just cried. And it can be very hard to talk during those times. Some of them are a thing of the past, as I have grown up and learned to cope, yet they still affect me completely. That's all that the people in that documentary notice. Just the outbursts, not the cry for help inside that you just can't get out. Not the mind going a million miles a minute and not the person trapped inside of it. And definitely not the things that they have done that have gotten you to that point.

However, the rest of the documentary counteracted all those claims and talked about the beauty of these minds that a lot of people don't understand. Things like learning to say the alphabet backwards at the age of two, memorizing all 900 songs on my iPod and phone word for word, keeping track of dates after only hearing them once, knowing people's birthdays like the back of my hand, having thousands of pictures coded into my brain and being able to see them like I was looking at the real thing, learning things about people by engraving it into my brain and being able to pull that information out at any second, knowing every word to my favorite movie making me able to watch it in my head, and remembering things said to me like they were just said two minutes ago. It's not just the anxiety, the perseveration, the stimulation, the awkwardness, the confusion, the tears, the long nights, the horrendous mornings, the lack of sleep, the lack of eating, the meltdowns, and the silence. It's not the years of misdiagnosis and traveling up and down the state to be told they didn't know what could possibly be wrong. It's the signature signed twelve years ago that finally saw me for what I was: autistic.

It shouldn't be trying to fit myself into this perfect little box and wanting all of it to go away so that I won't be different. It needs to be accepting myself for who I am and who I was put on this earth to be. It shouldn't be filled with shame of things that I can't change, but it should be filled with pride for how much I have overcome. And yes, there are still fears about the most important aspects of my future. Will I be able to be a teacher? Will I be able to be a mom? Will my kids inherit this from me? But as long as I have acceptance in my heart, and the same supportive people in my life that I have today, I will be able to do anything I set my mind to.

This is what autism means. And sometimes it looks just like me.